Joseph Fitzgerald Molloy

The Life and Adventures of Edmund Kean

Vol. 2

Joseph Fitzgerald Molloy

The Life and Adventures of Edmund Kean
Vol. 2

ISBN/EAN: 9783337339203

Printed in Europe, USA, Canada, Australia, Japan

Cover: Foto ©Thomas Meinert / pixelio.de

More available books at **www.hansebooks.com**

THE LIFE AND ADVENTURES

OF

EDMUND KEAN

TRAGEDIAN.

1787—1833.

BY

J. FITZGERALD MOLLOY,

AUTHOR OF

"THE LIFE AND ADVENTURES OF PEG WOFFINGTON";
"COURT LIFE BELOW STAIRS, OR LONDON UNDER THE GEORGES";
"ROYALTY RESTORED, OR LONDON UNDER CHARLES II.";
"FAMOUS PLAYS," &c.

IN TWO VOLUMES
VOL. II.

London:

WARD AND DOWNEY,
12, YORK STREET, COVENT GARDEN, W.C.
1888.

[All rights reserved.]

Richard Clay & Sons, Limited,
London and Bungay.

CONTENTS OF VOLUME II.

CHAPTER I.

Junius Brutus Booth—Extraordinary resemblance to Kean—A youth of many parts—Engaged for Covent Garden—Amazement and enthusiasm of the audience—Is visited by Edmund Kean—plays Iago to Kean's Othello—Disappoints an audience—Back at Covent Garden—Refused a hearing—Excitement of the town—Edmund Kean's letter—Booth plays Sir Giles Overreach—Kean's fresh triumphs—Kemble's retirement—His last performances—Macready's dissatisfaction—Success achieved by Rob Roy—A new departure from an old custom—Miss O'Neill's marriage ... ... p. 1—41

CHAPTER II.

Kean goes abroad—His admiration for Talma—Stephen Kemble becomes manager of Drury Lane—His great bulk—Disastrous results of his management—John Howard Payne and his tragedy of *Brutus*—Douglas Kinnaird's suggestion to Kean—Drury Lane in debt—Kean offers to become lessee—Elliston becomes manager—Kean's letter to the lessee—Presentation of a sword to Kean by his admirers in Edinburgh—Preparing for the tragedy of *Lear*—Kean and

Buckstone—Compassion for distressed players—The noblest execution of lofty genius—Preparing to visit America—Farewell performance ... ... *p.* 42—71

CHAPTER III.

Kean's first appearance in New York—Encountering prejudice—Sought after in social circles—Dr. Francis gives his opinion—Acting in Philadelphia—Lion-hunters—Performs at Boston—Unpleasant occurrence—Letters to the papers—Erecting a monument to G. F. Cooke—Back in England—Entrance into London—Reconstruction of Drury Lane—An assemblage in mid-air—Engagement of Charles Young—Kean's letter to Elliston—Kean and Young play Othello and Iago—A little cloud ... ... *p.* 72—104

CHAPTER IV.

Edmund Kean and his son—A night drive—A day at Boulogne—a drama in real life—Alderman Cox and his wife—Joe Cowell's story—Evidence given at the trial—Kean's letters—Result of the action—Kean determines to face the public—A Visit from Elliston—Storms at Drury Lane—Behaviour of the press and the public—Kean resolves to visit America—Eccentricity of his conduct—His condition at this period—Meeting with J. B. Booth—Booth's eccentricities—His adventures in America—Life at the farm *p.* 105—153

CHAPTER V.

An eventful year for Edmund Kean—Before a New York audience—Behaviour of the house—An appeal to the public—Excitement at Boston—Riot in the theatre—A stormy night—Kean makes his escape—Conduct of the mob—Back in New York—Phases of insanity—Playing at Philadelphia—Visit to Charleston—A wreck of his former self—At Quebec—Amongst the Indians—Made an Indian chief—Alanienouidet on his throne—Reception of Dr. Francis—Farewell to America   ...   ...   p. 154—177

CHAPTER VI.

Changes at Drury Lane—The new manager—Kean's reception by the public—Indications of ill-health—Grattan's tragedy of *Ben Nazir*—A morning visit to the tragedian—Studying his part—A painful performance—A shadowed life—Young Charles Kean—His engagement at Drury Lane—First appearance—Severity of the critics—Acting in Dublin—Three cheers for a speech—Edmund Kean in Paris—Reconciled to his son—Charles Kean plays Romeo—The elder Kean at Covent Garden—The cry of a despairing soul—At Bute—A pitiful letter—Quarrels with the management of Covent Garden   ...   .   p. 178—205

CHAPTER VII.

A new sensation in the theatrical world—The fate of Covent Garden—Fanny Kemble studies Juliet—In an empty theatre—Preparing for a first appearance—A memorable cast—Feelings of the new Juliet—Facing a crowded house—A blissful girl—Wonderful success and its results—An uncomely Romeo—In the provinces—Kean prepares to act Henry V.—Illness and postponement of the play—A pitiful sight—A melancholy letter—Fight for me—At the Victoria Theatre—A remarkable speech—Preparing to visit America once more—A memorable performance   ...   p. 206—239

CHAPTER VIII.

Robert William Elliston becomes lessee of the Surrey Theatre—Whimsical speeches to his audiences—Douglas Jerrold and his plays—Little Shakespeare in a camlet cloak—First production of *Black-Eyed Susan*—Elliston's last days—Charles Young says farewell to the public—Fanny Kemble bids good-bye to England—Charles Kean's struggles—Visit to America—Junius Brutus Booth at Orleans — Playing at Boston — Strange incident — His exit from life's stage—Edmund Kean at Richmond—Failing health—Helen Faucit's Recollections of him—His last performance—Reconciliation with his wife—His last days and his death ... *p.* 240—286

EDMUND KEAN.

CHAPTER I.

Junius Brutus Booth—Extraordinary resemblance to Kean—A youth of many parts—Engaged for Covent Garden—Amazement and enthusiasm of the audience—Is visited by Edmund Kean—Plays Iago to Kean's Othello—Disappoints an audience—Back at Covent Garden—Refused a hearing—Excitement of the town—Edmund Kean's letter—Booth plays Sir Giles Overreach—Kean's fresh triumphs—Kemble's retirement—His last performances—Macready's dissatisfaction—Success achieved by Rob Roy—A new departure from an old custom—Miss O'Neill's marriage.

Soon tidings reached the manager of Covent Garden, that a young actor named Booth, who in size, face, voice, and manner so strongly resembled Kean that he might be taken for his twin brother, was playing Richard III. at Brighton and Worthing with great success. Immediately it occurred to Harris that Booth might be produced as a counter-attraction to the Drury Lane tragedian, and he was therefore sought for and found, when an offer of appearing at Covent Garden was immediately made him, with a promise that if he were successful, an engagement should follow. And these terms being gladly accepted by him, arrangements were made for his *début*. In order to render this more attractive, rumours were spread concerning his extraordinary resemblance to Kean, which heightened the curiosity of the town to see him.

Junius Brutus Booth was born in Queen Street, Bloomsbury, on the first of May, 1796, and was therefore nine years younger than Edmund Kean. His father, who was a man of law, was likewise an admirer of literary genius in general, and of the scathing satirist who concealed his identity under the name of Junius in particular. And as Junius was likewise supposed to write under the name of Brutus, Mr. Booth, on becoming the father of a son, called him Junius Brutus, in memory of one he so much revered. On growing up, the lad, who was gifted with great versatility, desired to be a painter, and for some time studied art; he then entered the Navy, which he quitted to turn printer; later, he devoted himself to reading law, which he abandoned to become a sculptor; and finally he went on the stage. His first appearance is said to have been made in a play called *John Bull*, produced in a temporary theatre in a loft above a cow-house, situated in Pancras Street, Tottenham Court Road. He then joined Penley's company at Peckenham, and subsequently travelled with this manager to Ostend, Amsterdam, Antwerp, Ghent, and Brussels. Privations awaited the company in a foreign land, and after a year's absence Junius Brutus Booth returned to his native country a more experienced youth. He then played at Worthing and Brighton, where his remarkable likeness to Kean in person and manner created a sensation, and finally procured him an invitation to play in London. At this time he had not reached his twenty-first year.

On the 12th of February, 1817, he was announced to appear at Covent Garden Theatre in the character of Richard III. A vast crowd, drawn by curiosity to see his performance, filled the house; and as he entered, dressed after the manner of Kean in the same part, the audience was struck with astonishment at the strong resemblance he bore in complexion, stature, figure, and face to the Drury Lane actor. The surprise was increased by the similarity of the tones and sudden changes of his voice; his gestures, gait, and rapid movements; the methods of his entrances and exits, and management of his business, to those of Kean. The whole performance was indeed the most extraordinary imitation that could be conceived, and only lacked the genius of the original to render it equal to his. The audience, at first amazed by this daring copy of their favourite, was gradually won to applaud this ingenious youth, and frequently interrupted him to vent its admiration; and as the curtain fell the cheers which filled the theatre indicated the favourable impression he had made. On Mr. Abbott coming forward to announce the performance of the *Midsummer Night's Dream* for the following evening, he was interrupted by a universal shout of "Richard! Richard!" He then withdrew for a few minutes, and returned to state, the wishes of the house would be complied with, and Mr. Booth would repeat his representation of Richard the ensuing evening.

An assembly yet more dense and eager gathered to see him the following night; his reception was enthusiastic, his playing was heartily applauded, and the tragedy was announced for the following Monday, four evenings later, amidst signs of the liveliest satisfaction. Meanwhile, the question of salary arose. Booth demanded an engagement for three years, at fifteen pounds a week—a remuneration his success seemed to warrant, but which the manager, fearing the town would quickly weary of this novelty, refused to give, offering him instead eight pounds a week. This he indignantly declined, and refused to play on the evening for which he had been announced. Therefore, on that day no mention was made of him on the bills, and *Pizarro* was substituted for *Richard III*. Wrathful that no apology was offered for the change, and no explanation offered, the audience, before *Pizarro* began, called for the manager, who, on his appearance, stated that Booth had desired his salary should be fixed before he acted again, on which Harris told him it would neither be for his advantage nor the interest of the theatre the question should be then settled, and suggested it were better to wait until his success were more assured. The statement was interrupted with cries of, "You've driven him to the country again; you've driven him to Drury Lane," to which Harris responded, it was far from his wish that Booth should return to the provinces; he hoped the door of reconciliation was still open, and that all would be amicably arranged.

News of this rupture speedily reaching the ears of the Drury Lane committee, they rejoiced exceedingly; and immediately resolved to offer Booth an engagement in their company. Kean was requested to carry this project into effect, and accordingly drove to Booth's lodgings, and in a friendly manner assured his imitator the Drury Lane committee were willing to secure his services, as he would see if he entered the carriage, then waiting, and drove with him to the theatre. Delighted by the proposal, Booth expressed his gratitude for this friendly behaviour, accompanied him to the playhouse, and there signed an agreement to act such characters as were allotted him for three years, at an increasing salary of eight, nine, and ten pounds a week.

The same evening it was announced at Drury Lane that Booth would play Iago to Kean's Othello on the 20th of February, 1817. The excitement caused by this statement rose to fever pitch, and little else was talked of throughout the town save the coming contest, as it was considered, between these actors. One of the morning papers, which published a statement of his engagement, remarked, " It was somewhat singular that Mr. Booth's professional promotion is owing to the interference of Mr. Kean, whose uncommon liberality on this occasion is doubly gratifying, when it is recollected that some persons have elected Mr. Booth into the rival of our modern Garrick."

On the evening of the 20th Drury Lane Theatre was crowded to its utmost limits; expectation shone on would quickly weary of this novelty, refused to give, offering him instead eight pounds a week. This he indignantly declined, and refused to play on the evening for which he had been announced. Therefore, on that day no mention was made of him on the bills, and *Pizarro* was substituted for *Richard III*. Wrathful that no apology was offered for the change, and no explanation offered, the audience, before *Pizarro* began, called for the manager, who, on his appearance, stated that Booth had desired his salary should be fixed before he acted again, on which Harris told him it would neither be for his advantage nor the interest of the theatre the question should be then settled, and suggested it were better to wait until his success were more assured. The statement was interrupted with cries of, "You've driven him to the country again; you've driven him to Drury Lane," to which Harris responded, it was far from his wish that Booth should return to the provinces; he hoped the door of reconciliation was still open, and that all would be amicably arranged.

News of this rupture speedily reaching the ears of the Drury Lane committee, they rejoiced exceedingly; and immediately resolved to offer Booth an engagement in their company. Kean was requested to carry this project into effect, and accordingly drove to Booth's lodgings, and in a friendly manner assured his imitator the Drury Lane committee were willing to secure his services, as he would see if he entered the carriage, then waiting, and drove with him to the theatre. Delighted by the proposal, Booth expressed his gratitude for this friendly behaviour, accompanied him to the playhouse, and there signed an agreement to act such characters as were allotted him for three years, at an increasing salary of eight, nine, and ten pounds a week.

The same evening it was announced at Drury Lane that Booth would play Iago to Kean's Othello on the 20th of February, 1817. The excitement caused by this statement rose to fever pitch, and little else was talked of throughout the town save the coming contest, as it was considered, between these actors. One of the morning papers, which published a statement of his engagement, remarked, " It was somewhat singular that Mr. Booth's professional promotion is owing to the interference of Mr. Kean, whose uncommon liberality on this occasion is doubly gratifying, when it is recollected that some persons have elected Mr. Booth into the rival of our modern Garrick."

On the evening of the 20th Drury Lane Theatre was crowded to its utmost limits; expectation shone on every face; excitement rose to its zenith. Dramatists and critics, actors and managers, crowded the side scenes; men of taste and women of fashion filled the boxes; old playgoers thronged the pit; the gallery overflowed with Kean's fervid admirers, all alike awaiting the result of what was now regarded as a trial of strength. Such a circumstance as this had not happened in theatrical history since David Garrick and James Quin—the founder of a new school of acting, and the monarch of the old—fought for victory in this same house.

When the curtain rose the universal excitement was intense; all eyes were fixed upon the stage; and enthusiastic greetings having been given to the heroes of the night, silence settled over the house. Booth at first seemed nervously to shrink from the contest, but overcoming his dread, went through his part with courage, and was ever and anon warmly applauded. Kean's self-possession was, as usual, undisturbed. It was noticed there was greater firmness than usual in his tread, that his voice was more clear, rapid, and decisive, but only the light flashing in his eyes indicated the emotions passing in his soul. His peculiar habit of walking diagonally from the middle of the stage into a corner, and then going half-way across the footlights, was adopted by Booth, and two persons moving in this way in the course of a scene had a somewhat ludicrous effect. As the tragedy advanced Kean's power was gradually felt, whilst Booth's declined in proportion; when the latter ceased to speak he was lost amongst the subordinate characters, and it required an effort of attention to recognize him as one of the chief attractions of the night. Yet when he delivered his speeches he regained his position, and was warmly applauded.

Kean apparently reserved much of his strength during the first two acts; but no sooner, says Barry Cornwall, who was present, "did the interest of the story begin, and the passion of his part justify his fervour, than he seemed to expand from the small, quick, resolute figure which had previously been moving about the stage, and to assume the vigour and dimensions of a giant. He glared down upon the now diminutive Iago; he seized and tossed him aside, with frightful and irresistible vehemence. Till then we had seen Othello and Iago, as it were, together; now the Moor seemed to occupy the stage alone. Up and down, to and fro, he went, pacing about like the chafed lion who has received his fatal hurt, but whose strength is still undiminished. The fury and whirlwind of the passions seemed to have endowed him with supernatural strength. His eyes were glittering and bloodshot, his veins were swollen, and his whole figure restless and violent. It seemed dangerous to cross his path, and death to assault him. There is no doubt but that Kean was excited on this occasion in a most extraordinary degree; as much as though he had been maddened by wine. The impression which he made upon the audience has, perhaps, never been equalled in theatrical annals. Even the actors, hardened in their art, were moved. One comedian, a veteran of forty years' standing, told us that when Kean rushed off the stage in the third act, he (our narrator) felt all his face deluged with tears—'a thing, I give you my word, sir, has never happened to me since I was a crack—thus high.'"

At the conclusion of the play, both actors seemed exhausted from the extraordinary efforts they had made. Being called before the curtain, Kean led Booth forward. John Howard Payne, the author of *Home, Sweet Home*, who was in the theatre, says, "Kean seemed to enjoy Booth's success just as much as the audience did, and as he brought him through the proscenium door, you could see by the intelligent glitter of his piercing eyes, and the smile through the copper colour of the Moor's face, a sort of fatherly feeling, as if dragging an over-modest son to receive the honours of his success. The whole house seemed to feel it in this spirit, and when Kean conducted Booth back to the door, and then made one step forward to acknowledge the compliment offered to himself, I thought the applause would never stop." It was certainly a night to be remembered, as William Godwin "rapturously exclaimed" to Mr. and Mrs. Cowden Clarke on quitting the house.

Because of the extraordinary sensation the performance had created, it was announced for repetition on Saturday the 22nd, two evenings later. The struggle to secure places for this date was great, and in some cases a guinea was given for a single seat, an unusual circumstance in those days. The committee, eager to profit by this excitement, sought to increase the accommodation in the boxes and circle, and carpenters were employed to carry out the arrangements. The house was filled at an early hour on Saturday evening; the excitement was not less than it had been two nights before, and display of power such as had been witnessed on that evening was again ardently expected. But the time having passed for the play to begin, and the curtain not having yet risen, the audience became impatient, and shouts from the gallery and cries from the pit grew momentarily louder. At last a fear fell upon the house that something had gone wrong, and this impression was seemingly verified by the appearance of Rae, who was now stage manager. Advancing to the front of the stage, he begged leave to read a letter received from Booth; this ran as follows—" Mr. Booth presents his compliments to Mr. Rae, and begs to inform him that, from the excessive anxiety of mind which he has experienced during the past week, he finds himself so extremely unwell, that he shall not be able to perform this evening, and he has gone out of town to recruit himself." Rae added, that he had not received this note until between three and four o'clock that afternoon, when he at once went to Mr. Booth's house, that he might learn more particulars concerning him. On his way he had met a friend, who said he had left Booth at one o'clock perfectly well; and on reaching his house, Mrs. Booth stated her husband had complained of being unwell, and had gone out, but if he had left town she was not aware of the fact.

A sense of disappointment fell upon the audience, to relieve which, Rae stated that Kean had agreed to play Iago to his (Rae's) Othello; but to this arrangement general opposition arose, and calls were made for Kean to play Othello. This wish being acceded to, the play began, Kean being vigorously applauded throughout. Before it concluded the following letter from Booth was received by the committee—

"Gentlemen,

"In an unguarded moment I quitted Covent Garden Theatre (where the most eligible situation for the exertion of my professional talents was open to me) to go over to Drury Lane, where I have since found, and felt to my cost, that every character which I was either desirous or capable of playing was already in possession, and that there was no chance of my appearing in the same. What occasion, therefore, could you have for me, unless to crush any talent I may possess in its infancy? I have now seen through my error, and have therefore renewed the negotiation which was so unfortunately interrupted with the proprietors of Covent Garden Theatre, and have just signed a regular article with them for three years; consequently, I have no longer the power of appearing again at Drury Lane Theatre, and you will have the goodness to take my name entirely out of your bills.

"I have heard, Gentlemen, that your treasury has benefited considerably from my appearance on Thursday last; I ask no pecuniary recompense for it. I only request that you will not seek to persecute or molest a young man just entering into life, and who cannot afford either to be shelved (according to the theatrical phrase) at Drury Lane Theatre, or to be put into such characters as must infallibly mar all his future prospects. I have the honour to be, gentlemen,

"Your very obedient, humble servant,

"J. BOOTH."

Next day, Sunday, bills were posted all over the town, stating that Booth had entered into a new engagement with the proprietors of Covent Garden Theatre, where he would appear on the evening of Tuesday the 25th, in the character of Richard III. Astounded by this intelligence, the committee of Drury Lane issued circulars, in which the management declared it owing to the public to state, that on Monday the 17th instant Booth had signed an agreement, declaring he had no engagement with the Covent Garden proprietors, that all treaties with that theatre were at an end, and that he had requested his name to be taken out of the bills, which was accordingly done.

In answer to this, notices were circulated by the authorities at Covent Garden, setting forth that Booth, having played for two nights at their house, and being then in treaty for an engagement with them, the Drury Lane committee were bound to inquire if all agreements with Booth had really ceased before making him a member of their company. Believing they had a lawful claim on his services, the proprietors were about to take an action against him, when, through the medium of a friend who witnessed Booth's distress, the negotiation was renewed and terminated. Finally, the proprietors of Covent Garden entreated that Booth would not be made the victim of disputes between the two theatres, "his youth and inexperience alone having placed him in a dilemma, from which it is hoped the candour and liberality of an English public will rescue him."

To this statement, which appeared in the *Morning Post*, the following paragraph was appended—"The proprietors of Covent Garden Theatre have received a notification from a person who states that he was at a place called the Coal-Hole on Sunday last, where a club called the Wolves are accustomed to assemble, and that he heard the whole party pledge themselves to drive Mr. Booth from the stage. If such conspiracy really exists, it is severely punishable by law." This assertion, which was intended to attract sympathy towards Booth, and turn away the wrath which it was feared the public would visit on his head, was speedily contradicted by the landlord of the Coal-Hole, who declared the club mentioned as being in the habit of meeting at his house, had for many months ceased to exist. Moreover, Edmund Kean, indignant that such an insinuation should be cast upon the Wolves, addressed the following letter to the editors of the principal journals—

"Sir,

"I think it my duty, in justice to a society of which I once had the honour of being a member, to refute a most malicious piece of calumny. The Wolf Club seems to have been the foil with which the friends of the *rival theatre* have for the last two years parried the public censure against their unsuccessful candidates. I wish, therefore, through the medium of the public prints, to inform their *fears*, that such a society is no longer in existence, has not been for the last nine months, and when it was, the principals of the institution were founded in integrity and *universal philanthropy*. The misrepresentations with regard to this society laid before the public, rendered it unjustly an object of reprobation, and in acknowledgment of my duty to that public, I resigned it.

"With regard to Mr. Booth, that I have the highest opinions of his talents I gave proof when I recommended his engagement to the Drury Lane committee. If any one shall assert that I would, individually or accessorily, do anything detrimental to the interests of Mr. Booth, or any brother professional, I should be happy in person to tell the propagator of such a report that it is a falsehood.

"I remain, sir, with the greatest respect,
 "Your obedient humble servant,
  "EDMUND KEAN."

Public excitement concerning this affair was furthermore kept alive by a bill being filed in Chancery on Monday, the 24th of February, by the committee of Drury Lane Theatre, against Junius Brutus Booth and the proprietors of Covent Garden Theatre, for an injunction to restrain Booth from acting at any other play-house save Drury Lane; but next day, upon the petition of the plaintiffs, their bill was dismissed out of the court, upon their paying the whole of the costs.

The town awaited Booth's next appearance at Covent Garden Theatre with eagerness, and an immense throng crowded the house soon after the doors were opened.

From the appearance of the audience, it was gathered an exciting evening had set in. At half-past six o'clock the curtain rose, and Booth appeared dressed for the part of Richard III., on which a violent storm of mingled applause and resentment burst from every part of the house. The confusion was deafening; whistles were blown, sticks rapped on the ground, hats were waved encouragingly, fists raised threateningly, whilst opponents and supporters shouted at the pitch of their voices. The while Booth stood patiently on the stage, waiting until an opportunity was given him to apologize for the recent disappointment he had caused the public; but those who considered themselves affronted by his conduct were resolved he should not be heard. Having waited for some time, he bowed and withdrew. Fawcett, the manager, then came forward, but the uproar continued as before; he likewise waited until a hearing might be given him, but waited in vain. As he stood gazing at the storm a note was flung on the stage, which he knelt down to read by the light of the lamps; and presently a shower of missives was thrown on the boards, when he made a mute appeal regarding the impossibility of reading and answering so many communications. And as the tumult continued to rage with unabated force, he bowed and withdrew, without being able to address the audience.

The play now began, the actors going through the scene in pantomime, their voices being drowned by the clamour, which rose to fury on the entrance of Booth. After a few moments he came forward to address the house, but being again refused a hearing, he made his exit amidst a burst of groans and cheers. Soon he returned, attended by a standard-bearer exhibiting a placard, on which were the words, "Grant silence to explain." But this not having the desired effect, Fawcett came on, and ordering the standard-bearer to retire, took Booth by the hand, and by gestures implored the house to hear him. His efforts having no avail they then withdrew, Booth looking pained, fatigued, and depressed.

Again the tragedy began, but not a sound of the actors' voices was heard; and meanwhile several fights between Booth's supporters and his opponents took place in the pit, the house looking on with interest. In the middle of the second act, a player entered on the scene with a placard, stating, "Mr. Booth wishes to apologize," to which came a response, "No more lies, no more lies;" then Fawcett led Booth forward once more, but their appearance seemed to increase the confusion. Another placard was then exhibited, bearing the words, "Can Englishmen condemn unheard?" but it seemed as if nothing could now quell the storm. The play was then continued, and ended in dumb show to an accompaniment of howls, groans, and cheers.

When the curtain fell it was hoped a hearing might be obtained for the unfortunate victim of general displeasure, and again Fawcett led Booth forward; they were, however, received not only by frantic yells, but by showers of oranges and orange-peel, before which they retreated. At this demonstration Booth seemed quite overcome by grief. When the farce began, a man in one of the boxes addressed the house, and his words seemingly giving offence to his neighbours, a fight ensued. Then arose a general cry for the manager, who, on appearing, was asked to have the originator of the quarrel taken into custody; but Fawcett replied, "This whilst I am manager of the theatre I cannot do; if the person has offended you, it is in your own power to turn him out."

The farce was then continued, but at its conclusion the audience showed no inclination to depart. By degrees the lights were extinguished, but the excitement and noise were as vigorous as at the beginning of the evening. Finally, a general demand was made for the manager, and after considerable delay Fawcett again came forward, and was now allowed to speak. Despairing, he said, of prevailing on the audience to hear him, he had retired to his home, from which he had just been summoned. It was his duty, as well as his desire, to comply with any wish expressed by the house. He believed it was Mr. Booth they really wished to see. He had remained at the theatre until a very late hour, hoping they would be pleased to hear his explanation, but being disappointed had at length retired, "overwhelmed with affliction at having incurred their displeasure."

"Bring him forward!" shouted several voices, to which Fawcett answered, "It would be an act of cruelty to call him at this hour from his bed where he sought peace and rest after the excitement and worry of the evening." So far as respected himself, he added, he felt called upon merely to explain the conduct of the proprietors, which he was ready to do; the question between them and the managers of Drury Lane was now reduced to a point of law, and would be decided before the proper tribunal. For that decision he trusted the public would be content to wait; by it the managers must abide. His address was frequently interrupted by shouts of "Booth for ever! no shelving!

no Wolves!" It was almost midnight when he concluded and the audience dispersed.

Four nights later, Booth was again advertised to play Richard III. at Covent Garden, and at an early hour that afternoon the streets leading to the theatre were blocked by excited crowds; on the doors of the playhouse being opened a desperate struggle ensued for admission. A printed address from Booth was placed in every box, and liberally scattered over the pit. No sooner had the throng taken possession of the theatre than a repetition of the former night's conduct began. In the midst of cries of " No Booth!" and "Booth for ever!" a man in the pit hoisted a banner bearing the words, " He has been punished enough—let us forgive him," when an immediate rush was made at this man of peace, and his banner torn to pieces. Thereon other flags were raised with the inscriptions, "The pit forgives him; Hear Booth of old Drury Lane in his proper place; No persecution; We pardon him; Booth has done enough to appease John Bull; Contrition purchases forgiveness even from heaven; Beware of the artillery of Drury Lane;" and these expressions being irritating to Booth's enemies, free fights ensued, and kept the excitement at its zenith until the curtain rose.

No attempt was made to address the house, and the

actors, as before, went through their parts unheard. When Booth entered a laurel crown was flung upon the stage, followed by oranges liberally and forcibly contributed by the pit. Confusion and riot continued, no one present paying attention to the tragedy, until a standard-bearer came forward with a placard stating, "I have done wrong; I have made sufficient apology, and throw myself on the candour of Englishmen." This, together with the indications of Booth's distress, helped to disarm the malicious feelings of his opponents, and from that moment the opposition became gradually less violent. The tragedy being ended, the manager came forward in obedience to a general summons, and said, " May I not interpret the call on me as a request on your part to know what the play will be on Monday?" to which came a chorus of replies, "Yes, yes; give us Booth." "Then," he answered, "submitting to your commands, as I always do, I beg to announce that on Monday the play of this evening will be repeated." This statement was received with applause, mingled with a few hisses, and Booth's friends felt they had won his battle. The disturbance at the theatre had become so serious that the Lord Chamberlain intimated to both houses, if the present disorder continued, he would consider it his duty to prevent Mr. Booth appearing on either stage; fortunately no necessity arose for putting his threat into execution, as Booth was allowed to act Richard III. in peace on Monday night.

When the novelty of his personation of the crookbacked king had begun to wane, he was announced to play Sir Giles Overreach, the part in which Kean had created so powerful a sensation. His appearance in this character was awaited with interest, and on his coming forward as Sir Giles, the audience was again amazed by the startling likeness he bore to Kean. "His resemblance to the Sir Giles of the other house," says the *Morning Post*, "was most striking. Less marked when in close and direct comparison, at a distance from each other they seemed cast by nature in the same mould. This similarity extended to their minds, and consequently to their general style of action, and therefore few who, beholding Mr. Booth, could not have fancied that Kean stood in all his excellency before them."

The sensation his action created throughout was wrought to its highest pitch in the last scene by an effort at realism that produced a startling effect. One of the attendants who supported him concealed a small piece of sponge dipped in rose pink, which Booth at the proper moment secretly slipping into his mouth, pressed with his teeth, whereon the semblance of blood oozed from his lips, conveying the idea that he had burst a blood-vessel. The controversy which arose regarding the justification of this action helped to keep his name prominent before the public. But gradually all interest in him waned, and his imitations of Kean in the great tragedian's characters became wearisome when their novelty ended. And ceasing to draw houses, his name was but seldom seen in the play-bills, so that towards the end of the season he was almost forgotten, and his benefit merely brought him the sum of sixty-seven pounds ten shillings.

The while Kean was winning fresh triumphs at Drury Lane by his representations of Timon of Athens, Sir Edward Mortimer, and Oroonoko. The success which had first awaited him steadily continued; for the versatility of his powers, beauty of his conceptions, and force of his realizations crowded the theatre and delighted the town.

Soon after Kean had electrified the public by his representation of Sir Giles Overreach, John Philip Kemble, in an ill-advised hour, attempted to play the same character. The result was not less disastrous to the part than to the actor's reputation. Requiring, as it did, varied display of passion, great facial expression, and subtle nervous force, the part was unsuited to the "exhibition of elegantly disposed drapery," which was the great characteristic of Kemble's acting. "We never saw," says Hazlitt, "greater imbecility and decrepitude in Mr. Kemble, or in any other actor; it was Sir Giles in his dotage. He is the very still-life and statuary of the stage; a perfect figure of a man; a petrifaction of sentiment that heaves no sigh; an icicle upon the bust of tragedy." The audience, struck by the vast difference between the styles of the two prominent actors, hissed Kemble. He had been thirty-three years before the London public, and had thought of retiring; but this reception determined his course, and he resolved to give his farewell performances. His resolution caused little regret, save amongst the now limited circle of his admirers.

Macready felt anxious to see him in the round of characters in which he had once been considered great, to convince himself, by careful and patient observation, how far this actor's title to praise might be exaggerated by his followers, or his demerits magnified by his detractors. Accordingly, every night Kemble performed, the young player might be seen in the dress circle, whence an excellent view of the stage was afforded. On the night when Kemble played Cato, a favourite character of his, which had of yore drawn crowded houses, the theatre was but moderately full, and little enthusiasm prevailed. "But there was Kemble!" writes Macready, "as he sat majestically in his curule chair, imagination could not supply a grander or more noble presence. In face and form he realized the most perfect ideal that ever enriched the sculptor's or the painter's fancy, and his deportment was in accord with all of outward dignity and grace that history attributes to the *patres conscripti*... The tragedy, five acts of declamatory, unimpassioned verse, the monotony of which, correct as his emphasis and reading were, Kemble's husky voice and laboured articulation did not tend to dissipate or enliven, was a tax upon the patience of the hearers. The frequently recurring sentiments on patriotism and liberty, awakening no response, were listened to with respectful, almost drowsy attention. But, like an eruptive volcano from some level expanse, there was one burst that electrified the house. This was his great effort, indeed his single effort; and great and refreshing as it was, it was not enough so to compensate for a whole evening of merely sensible cold declamation. I watched him intently throughout,—not a look or a tone was lost by me; his attitudes were stately and picturesque, but evidently prepared; even the care he took in the disposition of his mantle was distinctly observable."

Very different was the exhibition which Macready witnessed a few nights later, when Kean played Sir Edward Mortimer in the *Iron Chest*. He felt that Kean had grasped a complete conception of the character, and was consistently faithful to it in every varying phase of passion. "Throughout the play the actor held absolute sway over his hearers," says Macready. "Alike when nearly maddened by the remembrance of his wrong, and the crime it had provoked, in his touching reflections on the present and future recompense of a well-regulated life, in pronouncing the appalling curse on Wilford's head; or when, looking into his face, and in the desolateness of his spirit, with a smile more moving than tears, he faintly uttered, 'None knew my tortures.' His terrible avowal of the guilt that had embittered existence to him brought, as it were, the actual perpetration of the deed before us; the frenzy of his vengeance seemed rekindled in all its desperation as he uttered the words, 'I stabbed him to the heart.' He paused, as if in horror of the sight still present to him, and following with his dilated eye the dreadful vision, he slowly continued, 'And my oppressor rolled lifeless at my foot.' The last scene was a working climax to a performance replete with beauties, that in its wildest burst of passion never 'overstepped the modesty of nature.'"

John Philip Kemble, continuing the representation of his famous parts, played King John, and Hazlitt records, he became the part so well in costume, look, and gesture, "that if left to ourselves, we could have gone to sleep over it, and dreamt that it was fine, 'and when we waked have cried to dream again.' In that prodigious prosing paper the *Times*," continues the critic, "which seems to be written as well as printed by a steam machine, Mr. Kemble is compared to the ruin of a magnificent temple in which the divinity still resides. The temple is unimpaired, but the divinity is sometimes from home."

On the occasion of his brother Charles's benefit, John Kemble, who was even yet called "the pride of the British stage," played Macbeth. To render the representation more remarkable, Mrs. Siddons left her retirement to act Constance, a part in which she had once thrilled the town by the force of her genius. But since those days time had in part robbed her of the powers which had helped to build her fame. The old fire and fervour had departed for ever, the once melodious voice had lost the fulness of its tone, the grandeur of gesture and grace of gait were missing; the poet's words were repeated with mere mechanical precision, and the tragedy dragged its slow way before a wearied audience.

On the 23rd of June, 1817, John Kemble made his last appearance. The house was crowded by those who for long had considered him a great actor, and were now anxious to testify their regret at his departure from the stage. The character he selected to represent on this occasion was Coriolanus, and his playing received the warmest applause. " The audience," says an elegant critic, " were obliged to chasten their exuberant delight by the recollection that the mental treat they were then enjoying was to be a last repast." When the curtain fell, loud cheers rang through the house, and in a few minutes Kemble came forward, seeming evidently moved by the enthusiasm he witnessed, and the ordeal he must endure in bidding the public adieu.

" Ladies and gentlemen," he said, in a husky voice, " I have now appeared before you for the last time; this night closes my professional life." Here he was interrupted by cries of " No, no," and after a slight pause he continued, with evident difficulty, " I am so much agitated that I cannot express with tolerable propriety what I wish to say. I feared, indeed, that I should not be able to take my leave of you with sufficient fortitude,—composure, I mean,—and had intended to withdraw myself from before you in silence; but I suffered myself to be persuaded that, if it were only from old custom, some little parting word would be expected from me on this occasion. Ladies and gentlemen, I entreat you to believe, that whatever abilities I have possessed,—either as an actor in the performance of the characters allotted to me, or as a manager in endeavouring at a union of propriety and splendour in the representation of our best plays, and particularly of those of the divine Shakespeare,—I entreat you to believe that all my labours, all my studies, whatever they have been, have been made delightful to me by the approbation with which you were pleased constantly to reward them. I beg you, ladies and gentlemen, to accept my thanks for the great kindness you have invariably shown me, from the first night I became a candidate for public favour, down to this painful moment of my parting with you. Ladies and gentlemen, I most respectfully bid you a long and an unwilling farewell."

Having bowed again and again in acknowledgment

of the enthusiasm which followed, he retired; but was immediately surrounded by his intimates and the members of his company, who awaited him at the wings. He then retired to his dressing-room, and distributed his costume amongst his brethren; to the facetious Mathews he gave his sandals, upon which that merry soul exclaimed, "I'm glad I got his sandals, for I'm sure I could never tread in his shoes."

A number of his followers, "humble votaries of an art he had so long ornamented, and enthusiastic admirers of the drama," resolved to mark his retirement by a farewell dinner, and the presentation of a piece of plate. Circulars were accordingly distributed, stating that tickets would be issued at two guineas each, which sum would include the expenses of the dinner and subscription to the testimonial; for these eager application was made. It was decided the testimonial should take the shape of a vase, for which Flaxman furnished a handsome design; commemoration medals were also struck for the occasion, and worn by the committee, bearing on one side a medallion of Kemble, and on the other the quotation, "Thou last of all the Romans, fare thee well." Thomas Campbell volunteered to write a valedictory ode, which T. Cooke set to music. This dinner was given on the 27th of June. On the morning of that day Kemble received a deputation from the Drury Lane company, represented by Rae, Dowton, Johnson, and Holland. The former, on behalf of his fellows, read an address, in which Kemble was styled the pride and ornament of the British stage; and reference was made to the dignity he had added to the profession by his genius, and the force of his example in private life. The dinner was given at the Freemason's Tavern, Lord Holland presiding. Kemble, in returning thanks for the honour those present had done him, spoke of the distinction they had conferred upon him, "such as had never been shown to any of his predecessors," and proposed the health of "the noble chairman." An address was read, toasts were drunk, speeches made, an ode sung, and then John Kemble's dinner was amongst the records of the past.

Meanwhile, Macready occasionally appeared at Covent Garden, but was wholly dissatisfied with the characters the management obliged him to represent. In a new play, called *The Conquest of Taranto*, he had been forced to accept the part of Valentio, "one of the meanest, most despicable villains that a romancist's invention ever teemed with." Willingly would he have paid the usual forfeit of thirty pounds as a consequence of rejecting a part given an actor by the manager, but the choice was not allowed him, and he regarded himself as "inevitably ruined by the exposure to such a degradation." During rehearsals he could not restrain his feelings, and when one day Booth, who was playing in the piece, told him he thought the part fully as good as his, Macready eagerly asked him to change with him, but Booth smiled and turned away. But on the night of the first performance of this play, Macready acted so conscientiously, that the interest of the principal scene shifted from Booth and centred in him; this being the reverse of what the author intended, and the manager expected, so that, instead of humiliation, Macready gained credit in the character. "This unlooked-for result," he writes, "ought perhaps to have acted as a lesson, teaching me for the future confidence in the ultimate triumph of careful and honest study."

In a play of Richard Lalor Sheil's, called *The Apostate*, he won another triumph, his representation of Pescara being so vehement, powerful, and truthful as to recall to Ludwig Tieck, for the first time since his arrival in England, "the best days of German acting."

But notwithstanding this success, he was soon after compelled to appear in a melodramatic afterpiece. Such occurrences hindering his ambition, and hurting his vanity, Macready began seriously to contemplate "some mode of escape from this distasteful and unpromising pursuit, and exchange it for one of greater utility." The only means of reconciling him to the calling he followed was the certainty of his gaining a place in its highest rank, and that seemed denied him. At this time, as in later life, he seems to have had little love for his art, and frequently appeared humiliated by what should have been his pride. There was, he records, small sympathy of taste or sentiment between himself and the frequenters of the green-room, "the conversation there being generally of a puerile and uninteresting character, and not unfrequently objectionable on other grounds." He therefore thought of abandoning the stage, taking his degrees at Oxford, and entering the Church; but the money necessary for this step he generously devoted to purchasing a commission in the army for his brother, and the meditated change was never made.

The opportunity for which he waited, though tardy in approach, was certain to arrive. In 1818 Pocock's musical drama, *Rob Roy Macgregor*, founded on Sir Walter Scott's novel of that name, was performed for the first time, when Macready as the Scottish outlaw won great applause. But it was not until the beginning of the season 1819 that the chance came which raised him to the position long desired. At this time Miss O'Neill was absent on leave until winter; Charles Young had quarrelled with the management, and gone over to Drury Lane; the only attractions remaining at this theatre were Charles Kemble, who in tragedy "spoiled a good face," and Macready. The season opened with *Macbeth*, Charles Kemble as the Thane of Fife proving a disastrous failure, to remedy which Macready was set forward in a round of characters that had won him good repute in the provinces. But he could not play nightly, and when absent the house was well-nigh empty. Ruin seemed inevitable to the managers, the actors were refused their salaries, and Harris told Sheil, "he did not know in the morning when he rose, whether he should not shoot himself before the night."

At this crisis Harris suggested that Macready should play Richard III., a proposal from which he naturally shrank, for Kean continually represented the part, and the younger actor, fearing comparisons, was reluctant to make the venture. Days passed, and the fate of Covent Garden Theatre grew darker still, when the manager told Macready the desperate condition of the house would "no longer admit of vacillation or coy timidity," and that he must appear as Richard III. He pleaded for time to read the part, but next day, in passing a Covent Garden play-bill, was amazed to find himself announced to personate the crook-backed king. With a sinking heart he went straight to his lodgings, knowing there was no escape, and prepared for the ordeal. He now devoted all his energies to the task before him; rehearsals were gone through with alternate feelings of fear and hope; old costumes were given him to dress the character, and for the alterations they required he was obliged to pay.

The 25th of October, 1819, was fixed as the date of the performance, and on the evening of that day a crowded house gave testimony of the interest with which the event was regarded. Then came the dreaded moment. The applause with which his appearance was greeted served to increase his nervousness; it seemed as if he were having a life and death struggle to save himself from ruin. The audience followed the first scene in silence; a whisper from a fellow actor, "it's going well," sounded as heavenly music in the tragedian's ear; then suddenly came a burst of hearty applause.

When Buckingham entered, Macready says, "I rushed

at him, inquiring of him, in short, broken sentences, the children's fate; with rapid decision on the mode of disposing of them, hastily gave him his orders, and hurrying him away, exclaimed, with triumphant exultation, 'Why then, my loudest fears are hushed;' the pit rose to a man, and continued waving hats and handkerchiefs in a perfect tempest of applause for some minutes. The battle was won." The excitement he succeeded in creating was maintained throughout, and when the curtain fell, cheers filled the house. On Richard III. being announced for the following evening by one of the actors, the audience would not hear him, but cried out for Macready, when the stage manager desired him to go forward; and this, it is noticeable, was the first time on which an actor came before the curtain at the conclusion of a play. From that evening the custom was adopted. Next day the press teemed with favourable notices of the performance; Covent Garden Theatre was once more crowded, and the actors received their salaries. Kean at Drury Lane likewise appeared in this tragedy, and the rival Richards became the talk of the town. Finally Mr. Harris senior, the patentee and chief proprietor of the theatre, made a journey to town from his residence at Belmont near Uxbridge, that he might personally thank Macready for the services he had rendered in rescuing his theatre from distress.

In the following month he achieved another triumph by his representation of Coriolanus, and his fame was finally secured by his personation of Virginius, a tragedy by Sheridan Knowles, of which a lengthy account is given in the pages of *Famous Plays*. He was now an established favourite with the town; the only tragedian of which Covent Garden could boast; the sole rival, Charles Young being set aside, of Edmund Kean. For his benefit at the close of the season Macready played Macbeth to a densely-crowded house. On this occasion he departed from a practice which had obtained for centuries; for up to this period it had been the custom for an actor on the occurrence of his benefit to receive monetary presents from his admirers; but to this habit, which seemed to compromise his independence, Macready objected, and he decided on not accepting a penny above the value of the tickets bought. He therefore returned various sums to the would-be donors, explaining to them his feelings on the subject, for "I could not," he says, "consider myself sitting down to table on terms of equality with a man to whom I had been obliged for the gift of five, ten, or twenty pounds."

Before this season ended, Miss O'Neill had ceased to delight the town by her graceful, sympathetic, and charming performances. During the five years that had elapsed since she made her first entrance on the London stage, she had accumulated the sum of thirty thousand pounds. On the 13th of July, 1819, she played Mrs. Haller in *The Stranger*, the occasion being announced as her last appearance before Christmas; it proved, however, her final performance to a London audience, for the year had not ended ere she retired from the stage, having married Mr. Wrixton Beecher, M.P. for Mallow, Co. Cork, who some years later inherited his uncle's baronetcy and estates.

Before accepting Mr. Wrixton Beecher as her husband, Miss O'Neill had outlived the romance of her life. Soon after she became known to the London public, she was surrounded by numbers of young men, the scions of nobility, whom her grace and her beauty attracted. Aware of the dangers that beset many members of her calling, she was guarded against their admiration, and was invariably accompanied to and from the theatre by her father or her brother. Her whole life was blameless, and so great was her delicacy, that she refused the manager's entreaties and commands to appear as Imogene, because the representation would involve the necessity of her appearing in boy's clothes. However, amongst those fascinated by her charms was a young man who quickly won her heart. Gaining assurance of his good fortune, he proposed to make her his wife, and he being the heir to an earldom, she might have been a countess; but before complying with his wishes, she insisted on having his father's consent to the marriage. The earl, though dissatisfied with his son's choice, had nought to say against the actress, but requested that a year's engagement should precede their union, during which time his son should travel abroad, and hold no communication with the lady he intended to make his wife.

And being deep in love and strong in faith, they consented to the trial, believing time would be powerless to change them. They parted with promises of eternal constancy; but before many months had passed rumours came concerning the unworthy life led by the lover; to these Miss O'Neill, still firm in her belief, would not listen, though they were repeated again and again. Still she hoped, even while she feared; and at length, to satisfy herself of the truth or falsehood of the assertions made, she obtained leave of absence from the theatre, and, accompanied by her brother and sister, travelled to Paris, where the man she was pledged to marry then resided. Here she ascertained for herself beyond all doubt that the tales she had heard were facts, when she broke her engagement, and returned to England. Overwhelmed with grief, she fell ill, and so serious was her ailment, that for days she lay in the shadow of death; but eventually she recovered to battle again with life, to live for the future, and to forget the past.

CHAPTER II.

Kean goes abroad—His admiration for Talma—Stephen Kemble becomes manager of Drury Lane—His great bulk—Disastrous results of his management—John Howard Payne and his tragedy of *Brutus*—Douglas Kinnaird's suggestion to Kean—Drury Lane in debt—Kean offers to become lessee—Elliston becomes manager—Kean's letter to the lessee—Presentation of a sword to Kean by his admirers in Edinburgh—Preparing for the tragedy of *Lear*—Kean and Buckstone—Compassion for distressed players—The noblest execution of lofty genius—Preparing to visit America—Farewell performance.

WHILST these events took place Edmund Kean still played at Drury Lane, now repeating his famous characters, again appearing in some dramas, which, from their unsuitableness to the stage, were signal failures. Amongst these were *Manuel*, a tragedy by Maturin; a dramatic version of Lord Byron's *Bride of Abydos*; and a tragedy named *The Duke of York*, compiled from Shakespeare's *Henry VI*. Kean also acted Achmet in *Barbarossa*, and Barabbas in *The Jew of Malta*, neither of which representations added to his reputation.

At the close of the Drury Lane summer season, 1818, he and his wife went abroad. In Paris he met Talma, who during a recent visit he had made to London, proved one of Kean's most ardent admirers. " He is a magnificent uncut gem," the French actor had said ; " polish and round him off, and he will be a perfect tragedian." To celebrate Kean's arrival in Paris, Talma gave a banquet to which the most prominent members of the Theatre Française were invited, when Kean was presented with a gold snuff-box. His enthusiasm regarding Talma's acting was great; he had seen nothing, he declared, to equal his representation of Orestes, and he resolved to play the part on his return to England. Leaving Paris, he travelled to Geneva, ascended Mont Blanc, and spent a night in the Hospice of St. Bernard. Here the calm and secluded lives of the monks, far removed from excitement and strife, forcibly impressed his sensitive nature ; and making friends with them, he sang to them, accompanying himself on a spinet, told them anecdotes of his life, described to them the world of which they knew nought, and finally took his leave with regret.

In September he was back in London, and on the 28th of that month appeared as Richard III. With the opening of this season Stephen Kemble, brother of

John Philip and of Mrs. Siddons, became manager of Drury Lane Theatre under the direction of the committee. Time was when Stephen, a mild-mannered, merry-hearted man, had played leading parts at Covent Garden. True, his engagement was made in error, he having been mistaken for his brother John,—then unknown to fame,—but his chance was given him, and availed him little, for Stephen was not an actor of merit. Having left Covent Garden, he returned to the provinces, and became manager of the theatre at Newcastle, where he married and settled. As years passed, he increased in size to such extent, that he weighed over eighteen stone, and when seated occupied three chairs at once. His bulk made him the butt of the theatre, and Oxberry used to narrate that one day when Stephen was passing through the meat-market he was beset by the butchers asking him, "What d'ye buy? what d'ye buy?" foreseeing in him, as they imagined, a profitable customer. But Stephen mildly replied he wanted nothing, and waddled peaceably onward until one man, more enterprising than his fellows, rushed from behind his stall, and eyeing Stephen's enormous person, said, "Well, sir, though you say you don't want nothing, only say you buy your meat of me, and you'll make my fortune."

Being appointed to his post at Drury Lane, for which he was by no means suitable, he brought with him his son Henry, whom he introduced as a new Romeo, much to the amusement of the town and the injury of the theatre. His management being influenced by economy, he gathered round him a company whose salaries were not calculated to press heavily on the treasury. The result proved disastrous. Rae, who was still at the theatre, was kept in the background, to make place for Henry Kemble, so that on nights when Kean rested, no attraction was held out to the public. In vain Stephen sought to fill the empty pit and boxes by producing a new piece every fortnight, one of them being written by himself, but all of them failed to attract. The manager now resolved to see if an exhibition of himself would draw the town, and accordingly advertised *Henry IV.*, in which he was to play Falstaff, " without stuffing," said the bills; but as his representation was devoid of humour, he was not a success. Failing to be a host in himself, he introduced a stripling to play lead, his sole recommendation being that he was a friend of Henry Kemble's. This youth, Hamblin by name, was a failure; and notwithstanding that the prices of admission to the house were reduced, the theatre was, save when Kean played, almost empty;

nay, even many who had orders given them could not be induced to attend the dull performances provided.

Naturally the committee was disheartened; new stars were sought and found in the persons of Cleary, Williams, and Sampson, who made first appearances in tragedy and comedy, and were scarce heard of more. A fairly good audience could be secured whenever Kean acted, but by constant repetition of his old characters, the interest in his playing had greatly decreased, and the houses he attracted were by no means comparable to those he had drawn a couple of years previously. The town, ever fond of variety, desired to see him in new parts, and on his return from Paris he had played Orestes in *The Distressed Mother*, but the result proved disappointing to himself and to his warmest admirers.

The affairs of the theatre became depressing, and ultimately the treasury was unable to pay the actors' salaries. As a last resource, the manuscript of an historical play called *Brutus, or the Fall of Tarquin*, by John Howard Payne, which had lain neglected and unread, was taken from a shelf in the manager's room, dusted, cast, and put in rehearsal, Kean having been persuaded to play the leading part. The author of this tragedy was, as in those times became one of his craft, a prisoner in the Fleet; but by the grace of "a day-rule," was enabled to attend the theatre, and communicate his ideas regarding the characters to the performers, and especially to Kean; though it often happened, when he had walked to Drury Lane to meet the tragedian by appointment, the latter was not to be found, or, pitiful to narrate, was not in a condition to be seen. At last *Brutus* was announced for performance, and on the first night of its production was almost damned; for Henry Kemble, weak and incompetent as a Tarquin, was hissed off the stage, and the play was only saved by Kean's outbursts of pathos and passion. The tragedy was repeated several times throughout the season, and so gratified was Kean by this result, that he presented a gold snuff-box, bearing on its lid the last scene from *Brutus*—not to the author, but to Stephen Kemble. Poor Payne received one hundred and eighty-three pounds for his tragedy, which brought the theatre ten thousand pounds.

But this one success could not save the house from impending ruin. The committee were still seeking for some novel attraction, when Mr. Douglas Kinnaird proposed Kean should play Joseph Surface. The part was accordingly forwarded to the tragedian, then fulfilling a brief engagement at Edinburgh, with a request that he would study it immediately. Kean's indignation at being asked to represent a part of secondary importance in *The School for Scandal* was such that he at once replied—

"Mr. Kean returns to the committee the character of Joseph Surface, which he has with surprise and mortification received this day. Mr. Kean wishes submissively to bring to the recollection of these gentlemen, that the material service which he has rendered to the establishment over which they preside has been by peculiar success in the first walk of the drama; and he will never insult the judgment of a British public by appearing before them in any other station but the important one to which they have raised him. It will likewise be impossible that he can reach London by the 4th, unless by breaking engagements and losing hundreds. But however arbitrary and unjustifiable the summons, he knows his engagement, and must submit. But he wishes them perfectly to understand, that, whatever is the consequence, he will not submit to any sacrifice of his talent."

To Douglas Kinnaird his letter was even more severe.

"Do you think, Mr. Kinnaird," he writes, "that ratified engagements are to be broken on a word? According to such principles I might say, I will not come to town for these two months, but knowing these affairs a little better than you do, I say I shall immediately come to London on the expiration of my Plymouth engagement, the 31st of August. Then I shall be compelled to give up situations that would have procured me hundreds. I have, with the just indignation of insulted talent, returned Joseph Surface to the committee. I cannot conceive their intentions towards me, unless it is to destroy my reputation as an actor, and interest as a man. But without disguise or subterfuge, I tell them—I'll be damned if they do either."

Some months later, through the failure of several pieces, and general mismanagement, the theatre was heavily in debt, and the committee were obliged to close its doors three weeks before the time when the season usually ended. It was now wisely resolved by them to withdraw from further interference with theatrical affairs, and let the house. Notices of their design, together with rules under which they were prepared to give up the theatre, were printed and circulated; and these reaching Kean, then on a professional tour, he felt anxious to become lessee, and from Harwich wrote the following letter to the secretary of the committee—

"Put down my name for a hundred pounds in the Drury Lane Theatre subscription list. I have received the conditions of the sub-committee, which nothing but madness could have dictated, or folly induce a man to read a second time. These are my proposals. I offer eight thousand pounds per annum for the Theatre Royal in Drury Lane, and its appurtenances, scenery, dresses, chandeliers, books, &c. &c. In a word, I shut my doors against all committees, expecting an immediate surrender of their keys and all privileges in possession. I select my own officers, my own performers, —'My reason's in my will,'—and can only be accountable to the proprietors for payment of the rent, and to the public for their amusements. This is my offer—if they like it, so; if not, farewell. Read this aloud to the proprietors, and as much in earnest as I write it."

Not satisfied with this epistle, he presently wrote another from Leeds.

"Sir, it was a saying of Aristippus, that it is a foolish thing to eat more than we can digest, the truth of which I am now proving; for really the printed articles of the agreement between the lessee and the proprietors of Drury Lane Theatre appear to be so indigestible, that the more I read the more I am constipated. They present a chaos from which my shallow brain, *talpâ cæcior*, perhaps, can extract nothing. To re-open Drury Lane Theatre under an experiment so obligatory would only plunge it into deeper involvements and more absolute contempt.

"The public has witnessed the mismanagement that has brought this magnificent theatre to ruin; its restoration can only be achieved by a popular professional man. I now stand forward to devote my property, reputation, and experience to this great cause—to cleanse the Augean stable, and 'raise a new Palmyra.'

"I cross the Atlantic should the proprietors reject my proposals, which are these—rent and taxes ten thousand pounds a year. The committee may pay my watchmen and firemen (persons in whom they place so deep a trust) if they please; but no servant except my own shall have ingress on my property. I shall propose such securities as the committee cannot think objectionable. Now, sir, everything else I reject *in toto*. Read this to the committee with emphasis and discretion. I have seen and known their errors; the world has seen and known them too. *Et vitio alterius, sapiens emendat suum.* Let me hear from you immediately, that in the one case I may be making my arrangements for the restoration of Drury's monarchy, or be preparing for crossing the Atlantic."

In his anxiety to become lessee he likewise wrote to Stephen Kemble. Between them a friendly spirit had ever existed, and Kean on one occasion, in comparing the manager to his brother, said, "Stephen has a soul under that load of fat which will ooze out; but John's is barred up by his ribs—a prisoner to his prudence." He instructed Stephen to state on his behalf, that if he obtained a lease of the theatre for ten years, at eight thousand a year, he would narrow the stage, which he then considered too wide, bring forward the boxes, and generally reduce the interior of the house, which was over large for sight or sound. Stephen added that the fact of Kean becoming proprietor would be hailed by the public with pleasure, whilst the performers believed him the most eligible person to manage the establishment.

Before the theatre could be let twenty-five thousand pound must be obtained to clear its present incumbrances, and it was therefore resolved, a voluntary subscription to raise the required sum should be opened amongst the shareholders, but they not giving so freely as was expected, the public were invited to contribute likewise. This drew down the wrath of the *British Stage.* "The impudence of these sturdy beggars is most surprising," says that publication. "What claim they can have upon the generosity of the public beyond any other set of bankrupts we are quite unable to discover. 'Tis true, that grievous forebodings have been heard of the sad injury which the drama will sustain, unless these silly speculators are helped out of the scrape into which they have plunged themselves; but though this may serve to gull a few simpletons, no man of common-sense will be deceived by it. The drama is indeed in a sad condition if its existence is inseparably connected with that of Drury Lane Theatre. These gentlemen thought fit to embark their money in a hazardous speculation; year after year they entrusted the conduct of it to men whose incapacity for the occupation had become woefully apparent; and now they are utterly ruined, they appeal to the generosity of the town. Fudge!"

Eventually the sum required was obtained, and advertisements were issued, inviting tenders from those willing to rent the theatre. Amongst those who were desirous of becoming lessees were Thomas Dibdin, Samuel Arnold, Edmund Kean, and Robert William Elliston. The proposal of the latter to take the theatre for fourteen years, to expend seven thousand pounds on the building during that time, to pay eight thousand pounds rent for the first year, nine thousand for the second year, and ten thousand for the remainder of his term, was accepted. For security he gave certain freehold, copyhold, and leasehold estates, valued at twenty-five thousand pounds, and on the 7th of August, 1819, he was declared the accepted candidate.

The theatre was to re-open in September, and meanwhile, the new lessee was overwhelmed by applications for engagements. Recognizing Kean's worth, Elliston wrote hoping he would co-operate with the new management; but the tragedian, feeling disappointed at being outbid by Elliston, whose former treatment he had never forgotten, declared he would never act under his authority in any establishment whatsoever; and as regards Drury Lane Theatre, he would rather pay the forfeit of his bond—a thousand pounds—than enter the house under the present lessee. Elliston begged his reconsideration of the statement, probably made in a moment of excitement, offered him such concessions as he desired, and added, "I shall think it no degradation to play Cassio to your Othello." Kean, in reply, indulged in a somewhat satirical strain—

"Sir,

"I congratulate yourself and the public on your accession to the diadem of Drury Lane, wearied and disgusted as all sensible people must have been with the stultified dynasty of the last two seasons. The lovers of the drama will hail with rapture a minister to their amusements so transcendent in his art and so mature in experience as Robert William Elliston. With regard to myself, I expressed my determination at the close of the last season to leave England. My arrangements are made. *Cras ingens iterabimus æquor*—I quit the kingdom! This has not been kept a secret. On my return I may treat with you; but it will not be consonant with my feelings to act in any theatre where I have not the full appropriation of my own talents. But I shall allow the field open to my compeers, and heartily wish success to all aspirants—this for the sake of the drama, which should be immortal. I have prepared Mrs. Kean to answer any inquiries that may be necessary in my absence. *Richards* and *Hamlets* grow on every hedge. Grant you may have a good crop. Yours,

"E. KEAN.

"P.S. If I should go by water to the nether world, I shall certainly relate to our great master, you thought it no degradation to act his Cassio."

Whilst Elliston was in a state of uncertainty regarding

Kean, he received a note from Mrs. Kean, saying a letter had arrived that morning from her husband addressed to his solicitor, requesting the latter would tender the penalty of one thousand pounds, and receive his client's articles. She, however, took the liberty of stating that Mr. Kean's friends had prevailed on him to continue his engagement at Drury Lane, and begged Mr. Elliston would write her a few lines mentioning what time he wished to meet her husband.

Whilst Drury Lane play-house remained closed Elliston had the interior handsomely decorated, and to inaugurate the new management, invited two hundred guests to a ball held in the theatre, when the stage was devoted to dancers, and the salon converted to a supper-room. Elliston having secured a competent company of tragedians, comedians, and singers of ballad operas, opened on the 4th of October, 1819, with *Wild Oats*, and an after-piece called *Lock and Key*.

Whilst in Edinburgh in October, Kean had amongst other characters represented Macbeth in a manner greatly delightful to his audiences; so gratified indeed by his performance were they, that several of these worthy citizens resolved on giving him a pledge of their appreciation, and selected as the most appropriate a sword of antique fashion and Highland make, ornamented with some of the most valuable precious stones which Scotland produces. On one side the blade was engraved the words, "To Edmund Kean, Esq., as a tribute of admiration of his splendid talents from his friends at Edinburgh;" and on the other side, "This sword was presented to Edmund Kean, Esq., to be worn by him when he appears on the stage as Macbeth, King of Scotland, November, 1819."

This was forwarded him on behalf of the subscribers by Sir John Sinclair, who in the accompanying letter said, the tragedy of *Macbeth* was the greatest effort of dramatic genius the world had yet produced, "and none have hitherto attempted to represent the Scottish tyrant who has done, that could possibly do, more justice to the character than the gentleman to whom I have now the honour of addressing myself." He added to the interest of the letter by stating, there was reason to believe Shakespeare collected materials for the tragedy of *Macbeth* on the spot where many of the incidents took place. "It is recorded," he states, "in Guthrie's *History of Scotland*, that Queen Elizabeth sent some English actors to the court of her successor James, which was then held at Perth, and it is supposed that Shakespeare was one of the number. The idea receives strong confirmation from the following striking circumstance. The castle of Dunsinane is situated about seven or eight miles from Perth. When I examined some years ago the remains of that castle, and the scenes in its neighbourhood, I found that the traditions of the country people were identically the same as the story represented by Shakespeare; that there was but one exception. The tradition is, that Macbeth endeavoured to escape when he found the castle no longer tenable. Being pursued by Macduff, he ran up an adjoining hill, but instead of being slain in single combat by the Thane of Fife (which Shakespeare preferred, as being a more interesting dramatic incident), the country people said that in despair he threw himself over a precipice, at the bottom of which there still remains the Giant's grave, where it is supposed Macbeth was buried."

Kean received the gift with great delight, and thanked his friends in grateful terms. On his return to London he made his appearance on the Drury Lane stage as Coriolanus, but the character being wholly unsuited to him, his performance was far removed from a success. This unsatisfactory result of great pains and careful study irritated him somewhat unreasonably against the new management; and a few nights later, an oversight on the part of a printer gave him an opportunity of threatening to free himself from a contract which he deemed a bondage. He had long since made it a point that his name should appear on the play-bills in letters larger than those of any other actor; and on renewing his engagement to the committee in January, 1818, a special clause guaranteed that his name "should be continued in the bills of performance in the same manner as it is at present." Now it was known Elliston wished to have the names of all the company printed in the same size, but was obliged to grant Kean's desire on this point. One evening, however, the tragedian's name appeared in the same type as that of the other performers, and next morning a note from his solicitor informed Elliston the contract between actor and manager had been cancelled by this breach of agreement. Elliston hastened to explain the compositor was alone responsible for the error, which he hoped would never occur again, expressed his regret, and finally succeeded in convincing Kean this departure from the usual custom was not intended as an affront. Thereon peace was made, and the tragedian prepared for his first representation in London of King Lear.

In consequence of the madness of George III., the performance of this great tragedy concerning a distraught monarch had for long been prohibited to the stage; but the record of His Majesty's miserable life ending after a seclusion of many years, on the 20th of January, 1820, the interdict was removed, and the play announced for representation at Drury Lane. Great were the expectations with which the public looked forward to the occasion, and many were the preparations made for the event by the management. Kean had long desired to act the part, in which he felt his great powers would find a fitting task. He now carefully studied the character of the grief-stricken Lear, and frequented St. Luke's and Bethlehem lunatic asylums, that he might observe the effects of madness before simulating it on the stage. In these days it had been the custom to present this fine tragedy as mangled and destroyed by Nahum Tate. Betterton, Garrick, and Kemble had acted this version, in which Edgar is made the lover of Cordelia, on whose union the king, recovering his wits and his kingdom in the last act, bestows a nuptial blessing. Unfortunately, Kean followed the example of his predecessors in playing this travestie, which Elliston must furthermore alter so as to make Shakespeare presentable to the public. Accordingly, the manager might be found daily in his private room at the theatre, his coat exchanged for a dressing-gown, his hair thrust up from his forehead, and standing out from his head after the manner of a tragic poet in a moment of inspiration, a pen behind his ear, another in his mouth, and on the desk before him a quire of paper, beside an open folio of Shakespeare. *King Lear* was subsequently published, and sold by the fruit-women of the theatre, as "adapted to the stage by Robert William Elliston, Esq."

Being accustomed to cater for the taste of the Surrey and the Olympic audiences, Elliston resolved to bring out *Lear*, with all the melodramatic display the tragedy would by the fullest licence admit. To the production of the storm scene his ingenuity was particularly directed. Some time before he had seen a mechanical exhibition, in Spring Gardens, by means of which striking scenic effects were imitated, which he believed would prove successful at Drury Lane; but on trial the machinery was found worthless on account of the great size of the stage. However, a hurricane he must have, and eventually he succeeded in obtaining a scene described in the bills as, "after the celebrated picture by Loutherburg of a storm on land." For this he had monstrous billows painted, and trees erected which swayed backwards and forwards with a creaking sound, the boughs of each having separate leaves that rustled in the wind. Every machine in the theatre capable of spitting fire, spouting rain, or bellowing thunder was pressed into service, whilst overhead were revolving prismatic coloured transparencies that cast continually changing supernatural tints, supposed to contribute to the weird character of the situation. The result on the first night was not all the judicious could desire, for King Lear for one instant was seen in a pea-green light, in the next in pale blue, and occasionally, in the event of a momentary cessation of the rotatory motion of the lantern, his head was bathed in purple, whilst the lower part of his body was suffused in crimson. Moreover, the noise of this stage storm was overwhelming— for the carpenters and scene-shifters, each working his sheet of thunder or his rain-box, together with the creaking boughs and rustling leaves, caused such confusion that no word the dethroned monarch spoke could be heard, and the tempest was subdued on the following night by general request.

Before the tragedy was produced, Kean requested a short leave of absence, that he might retire into the country, and make himself perfect in his part. He therefore went to Hastings, and every day strode backwards and forwards upon a lonely part of the beach reciting his lines. On more than one occasion he was irritated to find his words were not merely addressed to empty air, for his solitude was shared by a companion, a lad who attentively read a book, from which he continually looked up to repeat its contents. At last, overcome by curiosity, Kean approached his companion, and addressing him, said—

"My young friend, I see you are much interested by what you read; may I ask the name of your book?"

The lad handed it to him, and Kean, to his surprise, saw it was a melodrama then being played at the Surrey Theatre.

"I see you have a taste for dramatic literature," said the great man; in reply to which the youth informed him his name was John Buckstone, and that he was a member of a theatrical company then staying at Hastings. Kean remarked he was fond of the stage himself, and liked Shakespearean tragedies.

"William Shakespeare," answered Buckstone, "is not a gentleman of my acquaintance, but I hope in time to be on speaking terms with him."

"May I inquire," said Kean, "what parts you act?"

On which Buckstone told him he had been engaged for general utility, that his company had been doing fairly well in this town until the arrival of Wombwell's

Menagerie, when the good people of Hastings had given their patronage to the wild beasts instead of to the poor players, a change which had caused great distress to the manager and his troop; for, playing to empty houses, they had received no salaries, and their only hope of being able to pay their debts and leave the town with their honour preserved lay in the benefit season, which was soon to begin. Kean expressed much sympathy, and stated his desire to see the theatre, which Buckstone readily offered to show him, and back they walked to the town, the lad hoping he had secured a patron.

But as they entered the street a post-chaise drove hastily by, in which Elliston was seated, and no sooner had the manager seen Kean than he stopped the horses and jumped out.

"My dear Kean," he said, "you must return with me to town; business has been ruinous this last week. I must announce you in one of your old characters."

Buckstone, hearing his companion's name, fell back with astonishment.

"But I came here," said the tragedian, "to study my new part."

"I know that; but I want you to return at once."

"Well, I will make a bargain with you," answered

Kean. "If you remain and play with me for the benefit of the unfortunate company here to-morrow night, I will leave with you next morning."

And Elliston agreeing to this, the *Merchant of Venice* was acted the following evening to a crowded house, and the players were not only released from pressing difficulties, but were in possession of a sufficient sum to carry them to Dover. In this manner did Buckstone, who subsequently became a famous comedian, make the acquaintance of Edmund Kean.

Before *Lear* could be produced at Drury Lane, Harris of Covent Garden announced the tragedy for performance on his stage. He had requested Macready to take the part of the king, but that actor, neither desiring comparison with Kean, nor willing to hurry through the study of a great part, promptly refused, stating at the same time he would appear in any other character in the play. Harris therefore engaged Booth, who had recently been performing at the Surrey Theatre, to act Lear, whilst Macready was cast for Edmund, and Charles Kemble for Edgar. It was produced at Covent Garden on the 13th of April, 1820, and proving a failure, was acted but three nights. On the 24th of the same month it was played at Drury Lane. The high anticipations entertained of Kean's performance were fully realized. In the first act his bearing and manner were majestic, without any approach to mock dignity; the rebuke to Cordelia, and his sudden change of intentions towards her, because of her apparent coldness, seemed the result of wounded pride in a monarch accustomed through life to have his will and wishes prevail in all things. His anger with Goneril was finely shown, and the curse was delivered with the tremendous force of his great powers. Throwing himself on his knees, he lifted up his arms, flung his head back, and breathed forth with awful solemnity and bitter woe this terrible and blasting prayer. The next scene has been described as the most finished of the whole performance, "and certainly the noblest execution of lofty genius that the modern stage has witnessed, always excepting the same actor's closing scene in the third act of *Othello*."

In counterfeiting madness his art was displayed in the highest perfection; his hands were as wandering and unsettled as his senses, and as little under the habit of control or will; his eyes in their vacant gaze or fierce light were terrible to behold. One critic declared Kean's performance as not unworthy of the character; and adds, "This is the highest and most comprehensive general praise that need, or perhaps can, be given to it; and nothing but this was wanting to fix and consummate Mr. Kean's fame. The genius of Shakespeare is the eternal rock on which the temple of this great actor's reputation must now rest, the 'obscene birds' of criticism may try in vain to reach its summit and defile it; and the restless waves of envy and ignorance may beat against its foundations unheeded, for their noise 'cannot be heard so high.'"

As will have been seen by his letter to Elliston, Kean thought of visiting America, an idea that gradually resolved itself into a decision. At the end of the summer season, 1820, his engagement at Drury Lane ended, and he was then free to transfer his services where he pleased. For his benefit on the evening of June 12th he was announced to appear for the first time as Jaffier in *Venice Preserved*, and as the Admirable Crichton in a piece bearing that name, written for him by Dibdin. As Crichton he was to sing, dance, fence, recite, give imitations of other actors, and finally play harlequin. That he who was capable of rousing vast audiences to enthusiasm and moving them to tears should condescend to cut capers as a harlequin, was an eccentricity which as sorely grieved his friends as it certainly delighted his enemies. On the night for which his performance was announced a great throng filled the house; not only was every available seat occupied, but numbers stood in the lobbies, hoping some chance would eventually give them a view of the stage.

Throughout the tragedy Kean's acting was powerful and pathetic, affecting and dignified, and the final scene roused the wildest enthusiasm. With mingled feelings the audience then waited for the after-piece. When the curtain rose again Kean was found seated at a piano, singing an original song, which was applauded and encored. He then fenced with his usual ability, and was victorious over his antagonist, a professor of the art named O'Shaugnessy. He next danced a *pas de deux* with Miss Valancy in a manner that drew cheers from the beholders; but suddenly he stood still, drew up one foot, and limped off the stage amidst great applause. This ended the first act. Before the curtain rose on the next scene, Russell the stage manager came forward and stated, that Kean having sprained his ankle in the last *pirouette*, it would be impossible for him to perform the part of harlequin as he had intended, but he would endeavour to continue the less laborious part of the entertainment. The drop scene being raised, Kean was discovered in a great arm-chair, from which he gave the imitations promised of John Kemble, sang after the manner of Charles Incledon, and caricatured Munden, Harley, and Dowton in a manner that caused universal laughter. The receipts of the house on this evening amounted almost to seven hundred pounds.

The season at Drury Lane ended on the 8th of July, but Elliston informed the public his theatre would re-open on the 15th of August, for the purpose of affording Kean an opportunity of playing his principal characters before his departure for America. And in order to give additional interest to the tragedian's farewell, Booth was engaged, and played Richmond, Pierre, and Iago to Kean's Richard III., Jaffier, and Othello. On the 16th of September Kean played for the last time in London before his departure for America. The character selected by him for the occasion was Richard III., and his acting was marked by its usual brilliancy and effectiveness. At the conclusion of the tragedy he was loudly called for, and came forward, seeming much agitated. The pit rose and cheered lustily, the gallery waved its hats and handkerchiefs, to which expressions of approbation he bowed repeatedly. It was not until several minutes elapsed that silence was obtained, and he was enabled to address the house. He then said—

"Ladies and gentlemen, it is with pain that I announce to you that a long period must elapse before I can again have the honour of appearing before you; and when I reflect on the uncertainty of life, the sentiment will intrude itself, that this may possibly be my last performance on these boards." Here he was interrupted by cries of "No, no, we hope not, Kean." He then continued, in a voice betraying great agitation —"I am unable to proceed. I cannot but remember with gratitude that this is the spot where I first enjoyed public favour. I was then a wanderer and unknown, but received here shelter, and, I may add, reputation. If ever I have deviated from that height to which your favour has raised me, it is to you only that I should apologize. During eight years your favour has been my protection and encouragement, my present enjoyment, my future hope. It has been to me a shield against the shafts of calumny to which I have been exposed; it is the cargo that freights my venture to another clime. Ladies and gentlemen, my heart is too full to add more. With deep sentiments of esteem and gratitude, I respectfully bid you farewell."

Before quitting London he gave a bust of himself to the theatre, which was placed on a pedestal in the principal green-room, the ceremony of presentation being followed by a supper to the company. From this pleasant gathering one was missing who had acted with Kean full many a time. Alexander Rae had made his exit from life's stage a little while before.

Kean performed some nights in Liverpool, whence, in October, he set sail for America.

CHAPTER III.

Kean's first appearance in New York—Encountering prejudice—Sought after in social circles—Dr. Francis gives his opinion—Acting in Philadelphia—Lion-hunters—Performs at Boston—Unpleasant occurrence—Letters to the papers—Erecting a monument to G. F. Cooke—Back in England—Entrance into London—Reconstruction of Drury Lane—An assemblage in mid-air—Engagement of Charles Young—Kean's letter to Elliston—Kean and Young play Othello and Iago—A little cloud.

On the last day of November, 1820, Edmund Kean made his first appearance in New York. The one theatre of which the city at this time boasted had been burned down the previous year, and the company had taken temporary refuge in a small house in Anthony Street. The excitement caused by his arrival had been great, many people travelling from Philadelphia to see him, and the building was crowded to excess. According to the *National Gazette,* no actor had ever appeared in New York with such prepossessions in his favour, or such prejudices to encounter; "and we candidly confess," says the journal, "we were amongst that number who entertained the latter. We were assured that certain imitations of him were exact likenesses—and that certain actors were good copies; that his excellences consisted in sudden starts, frequent and unexpected pauses, in short, a complete knowledge of what is termed stage-trick, which we hold in contempt. But he had not finished his soliloquy before our prejudices gave way, and we saw the most complete actor, in our judgment, that ever appeared on our boards. The imitations we had seen were indeed likenesses, but it was the resemblance of copper to gold, and the copies no more like Kean 'than I to Hercules.'"

Night after night a rush which well-nigh proved disastrous to many was made to secure places at the theatre, so that a notice was issued by the management, stating that in order "to prevent the riotous scenes which have disturbed the peace of the town in the vicinity of the theatre for several days and nights past, in efforts to forestall tickets, the managers have directed that the box-tickets and the whole lower tier, and fourteen of the second row next to the stage, shall be sold by public auction, the premiums from the choice to be appropriated to the Massachusetts' General Hospital." But though great audiences flocked to see him, so that the receipts of the theatre, which previously but amounted to a thousand dollars a week, now reached that sum nightly, the critics could not agree concerning the merits of his acting. One writer remarked, amongst other objections, that his "local pronunciation does him an injury in the country where we have the pure English." Of the censure or praise of the press Kean took little heed, satisfied that his efforts drew crowded houses, and gained him enthusiastic applause.

In social circles his society was courted by the most prominent and cultured citizens, amongst whom was John William Francis, a medical doctor, notable as an ardent admirer of genius, and a hospitable host of celebrities. In his interesting reminiscences, Dr. Francis has left us his impressions of Kean, for whom he entertained a lively friendship. "He won my feelings and admiration from the moment of my first interview with him," says the worthy doctor. "Association and observation convinced me, that he added to a mind of various culture the resources of original intellect; that he was frank and open-hearted, often too much so, to tally with worldly wisdom. I was taught by his expositions in private, as well as by his histrionic displays, that the great secret of the actor's art depends upon a scrutinizing analysis of the mutual play of mind and matter, the reflex power of mental transactions on organic structure. His little but well-wrought strong frame seemed made up of a tissue of nerves. Every sense appeared capable of immediate impression, and such impression having within itself a flexibility truly wondrous. The drudgery of his early life had given a pliability to his muscular powers that rendered him the most dexterous harlequin, the most graceful fencer, the most finished gentleman, the most insidious lover, the most terrific tragedian."

Examining his character, which he found to be of unusual versatility, and studying his genius, which he discovered to possess unsuspected capacities, Dr. Francis was charmed by the tragedian. The manners, habits, and customs of Shakespeare's age were familiar to him; he had studied phrenology, and was a physiognomist of rare discernment. "His analysis of the characters who visited him, to do homage to his renown, often struck me with astonishment." Intuitively he gauged the feelings of an audience the moment he appeared before them; he was curious in searching into causes; he could echo the warblings of birds, imitate the voices of beasts, and the peculiarities of his fellow actors; was a ventriloquist, and sang Moore's melodies with great feeling and much sweetness. He considered Shakespeare the hardest study to grapple with, but when once the poet's lines were fixed in his memory they remained there, whilst there were parts of modern dramas he could not retain. Though daily in his company, Dr. Francis states he never saw him look at the great dramatist's plays save once, when he was about to act King John; and though he seldom attended rehearsals, yet he never once disappointed the public, even "when suffering from bodily ills that might have kept a hero on his couch." He considered the third act of *Othello* his greatest performance, and he was proud of representing Shakespearean characters; "but he told me a hundred times," said his friend, "that he detested the profession of an actor."

Before leaving New York a public dinner was given him, and his health being drank, he expressed his delight in having such an excellent opportunity of offering, "in the simple language of the heart, my most grateful acknowledgments to the citizens of New York." When a professional man was fortunate enough to blend private esteem with public approbation, the speaker said, he might be considered to have attained the very extent of his ambition. The union of these feelings had been so manifest during his short residence in the city, that he would place their records in eternal memory. "Nor does the influence of your favour," he continued, "extend only to the stranger whom you have so generously welcomed. There are hearts conjoined to mine by ties of affection and alliance, which are this moment, perhaps, anticipating with joy my professional success in this country, and in which will arise a permanent sentiment of gratitude for the favour I have here experienced. It is there, gentlemen, in my domestic circle, that I shall dwell upon the retrospect of those hours; it is there I shall instruct the being entrusted to my care to respect and love the patrons of his father; and while the pages of your history record achievements that give lustre to the political and warlike character of your country, be assured that the English actor will, to the last hour, extol the merits of your private worth, and gratefully transmit his Columbian laurels to the charge of his posterity."

Leaving New York he journeyed to Philadelphia; but here, likewise, his reception by the press was not wholly favourable. The *Literary Gazette* murmured against "the foreign tragedian," who, "though sufficiently distinguished and exalted at home, is to be magnified and glorified here, for his own satisfaction and other discernible objects." The same paper, criticizing his Sir Giles Overreach, states he drew a considerable auditory, comprising as large a portion of the cultivated and acute understandings as would be found in any casual assemblage of like number in any other of our cities; and adds, that during the first four acts of the play no indications of strong emotion were given by the house, for "an uncommon apathy appeared to reign, considering the ordinary proneness to clapping, and the kindly mood which prevail whenever an actor of much celebrity is treading the boards."

But another paper, speaking of the same performance, relates that the audience was roused to the highest pitch of admiration, and cries of "Bravo" "bore testimony to the wondrous powers of this extraordinary man." His success will perhaps be better estimated from a statement made in one of his letters. "Everything," he writes, "both on and off the stage, in this country has exceeded my most sanguine expectations. I am getting a great deal of money, and all is going well. I am living in the best style, travelling magnificently, and transmitting to England a thousand pounds each month."

The manager of the Philadelphia Theatre, William B. Wood, in his *Personal Recollections of the Stage*, says Kean at once satisfied his audiences that his vast fame had been fairly acquired. "The verdict, however, was not perfectly unanimous; some determined critics, who had persuaded themselves that G. F. Cooke's loss was never to be supplied, were on the first night loud in condemnation of the new actor, whom they honoured with the names of quack, mountebank, and vulgar impostor. Strangely enough, his second appearance at once converted these judges into his most enthusiastic admirers. The little hero acted Richard III. with marvellous spirit, although upon his first entrance his agitation was so strong as to be visible to those near the stage." Kean's playing in Philadelphia led to a custom heretofore unknown in that city, but subsequently followed. "I allude," says Wood, "to the habit of calling out performers, dead or alive, after the curtain has dropped, to receive a tribute of extra applause. The absurdity of dragging out before the curtain a deceased Hamlet, Macbeth, or Richard in an exhausted state, merely to make a bow, or probably worse, to attempt an asthmatic address in defiance of all good taste, and solely for the gratification of a few unthinking partisans, or a few lovers of noise and tumult, is one which we date with us from this time. It has always been a matter of wonder with me, that the better part of the audience should tolerate these fooleries. Can anything be more ridiculous than that an actor, after labouring through an arduous character, a protracted combat, and the whole series of simulated expiring agonies, should instantly revive, and appear panting before the curtain, to look and feel like a fool, and to destroy the little illusion which he has been endeavouring to create."

Behind the curtain, as well as before, Kean created interest and surprise. A hundred stories concerning the Wolves' Club, his eccentric habits, his tame lion, his midnight rides, his visits to taverns, had preceded him, and the company at the Philadelphia Theatre were prepared to find him cantankerous, arrogant, and offensive; they were therefore happily disappointed at discovering him to be a mild, unassuming man, free from affectation of superiority. His suggestions regarding stage business were given in a manner that secured their immediate adoption; and the deficiencies of the humbler actors were treated by him with an indulgence that created in the most careless a desire to excel.

Wood narrates, that Kean's presence in the green-room was ever a source of enjoyment, and adds, "I speak of him and his deportment throughout a long series of performances. In private society, particularly in the company of ladies, he was distinguished for his modest and unassuming manner as well as conversation.

One of his weaknesses, and a cause of his ruin, was the allowing himself to be beset by a crowd of idlers, always found ready to attach themselves to the skirts of each new actor, singer, dancer, or equestrian. These thoughtless persons were in the constant habit of calling at the stage-door after the play, in order to waylay and carry him off to some late supper or party at the moment of extremest exhaustion from his labours. A protracted sitting and a late banquet were sure to leave him the ensuing morning weak and enfeebled. His strength of constitution, however, would enable him to rally for the night's exertion, too often to be followed by the same indiscretion. Unlike Cooke, who could bear two or three bottles of port wine, Kean would be overset by as many glasses. He was aware of his folly in submitting to these midnight wastes of time and health, but wanted firmness to resist them. I frequently remained with him in his dressing-room after performance for several hours, in order to tire out these persevering tempters, who would remain in their carriages at the stage-door with the most indelicate pertinacity. On one occasion we stayed inside the building until nearly three o'clock before the rumbling of the carriages announced the departure of his persecutors. It was impossible not to feel a deep interest for a man who, too weak to resist temptation, possessed sensibilities of conscience and character which brought the deepest contrition and shame on every occasion of offence."

From Philadelphia he journeyed to Boston, where he met with an enthusiastic reception, fully equal to that which Jenny Lind had experienced some time before. He was announced to play for nine evenings, and the rush to secure places for his first representation was so great, that the managers of the theatre, Messrs. Powell and Dickson, auctioned the tickets for the remaining performances, the premiums realized being given to charitable institutes in the city, every one of which benefited by the universal desire to see the famous actor.

On the 12th of February, 1821, he began his engagement by appearing as Richard III., and won the stormy applause of a large audience. His acting, fresh, vigorous, and natural, became the leading topic of conversation, whilst his society was eagerly sought after. Kean was delighted by the enthusiasm he created, the courtesy he received, and the reward his exertions gained. After the receipt of the first thousand dollars a week, he shared with the management, and had a clear benefit, so that he received for nine nights upwards of six hundred and thirty pounds. So great was his popularity, that he was then re-engaged for six nights at a salary of fifty pounds a night and a full benefit, which added a further sum of about four hundred and forty pounds. This additional stay by no means exhausted his popularity, for when at the conclusion of his last representation he was called before the curtain, there was a universal cry asking him to prolong his visit. For this he returned the house his hearty thanks, and regretted his engagements in the South prevented him from complying with its wishes, but should any circumstance arise of which he could avail himself to re-visit " the literary emporium of the new world," he would seize it with heartfelt satisfaction.

Three months later—early in May—having concluded his engagements in the South, Kean expressed his intention of again visiting Boston; whereon Dickson immediately wrote that this was the season when the better and wealthier classes were out of town, and begged him to postpone his re-appearance until autumn. But Kean, feeling fully satisfied he would draw crowded houses at any time, refused to act on the advice given him, and on the 23rd of May appeared upon the Boston stage as King Lear. Two nights later he played Jaffier, and though the receipts of both performances were devoted to charities, the audiences were not large.

On the third evening he was announced to play Richard III., but before dressing looked through a slit in the curtain, and saw there were merely about twenty persons present, on which he sought the managers, and told them he would not act to bare walls. Dickson strongly urged him to play that night, and keep his faith with the public, after which he would release him from his engagement; but Kean refused, saying he would leave Boston next morning; and inviting his manager to come out and have a parting drink, he took his departure from the theatre. But scarce had he gone when the boxes began to fill, and presently a fair house had assembled, word of which was sent him, with a request that he would return; but he peremptorily declined to act that night.

Meanwhile as the curtain remained down, though the hour for beginning the tragedy had passed, the audience became impatient, when the stage manager went forward and said, he felt regret and embarrassment in informing them that Mr. Kean had refused to perform that evening. He wished to know if those present would desire the play to proceed without Mr. Kean. To this question came an affirmative from all parts of the house; but when the curtain rose a demand was made for the stage manager, who, on appearing, was asked why Kean had refused to play. He replied, because the house was not crowded. The tragedy of *Richard III.* then began, and was allowed to proceed without further interruption.

Kean's refusal to act, being regarded by the Bostonians as an insult, created general indignation; and as he had previously been lauded, so was he now abused. The press taking the popular side, censured him, and incited the public to fresh wrath. The general tone of its remarks may be gathered from the following paragraph published in one of the leading organs—

"ONE CENT REWARD.

"Run away from the 'Literary emporium of the New World,' a stage player calling himself Kean. He may be easily recognized by his misshapen trunk, and his coxcomical Cockney manners. His face is as white as his own froth, and his eyes are as dark as indigo. All persons are cautioned against harbouring the aforesaid vagrant, as the undersigned pays no more debts of his contracting after this date. As he has violated his pledged faith to me, I deem it my duty thus to put my neighbours on their guard against him.

"Peter Public."

The New York journals likewise waxing wrathful over an action which they magnified into a grave offence, violently abused him, and so great was the animosity they succeeded in rousing against him, that Kean found it necessary to explain his conduct in a long letter addressed to various journals. He was anxious, he said, to preserve the good opinion of the friends who had generously and nobly manifested their approbation of his character and talents. He was aware he was amenable to public opinion and censure, and if the public voice declared he was in error, he was ready to apologize with all due submission. But he thought it extraordinary, that though the offence with which he was charged took place in Boston, with the concurrence of the manager and the approbation of his friends, he should have heard nothing of it until his arrival in New York, where "murmurs of disapprobation were heard, which appeared to me like an overwhelming avalanche at the termination of a brilliant harvest." He lived by his professional exertions; innumerable family claims were satisfied by each month's disbursements, and he could not afford to exert his talents without payment. He had represented two of his principal characters without hope of remuneration, in a town where three months before his efforts had contributed largely to augment the public charities. Seeing but twenty persons in the house on the night when he was to play Richard III., he had considered it better to husband his resources for a more favourable season, and in this decision no disrespect was contemplated towards the audience. "The managers," he added, "apparently concurred with me, deplored the unfortunate state of the times, and we parted in perfect harmony and confidence." The present hostility he would not believe was the voice of the public, but the spirit of detraction ever attendant on little minds—a spirit which watches for its prey, and seizes on transient and accidental occurrences to defame and to destroy. That the press of America should be influenced by such feelings, that they should denounce with such acrimony, was to him extraordinary. It had been his intention to leave America at the close of his southern engagements, but he would certainly return to Boston, and in person vindicate his cause during the season, when those who patronized the drama returned to that city.

In reply to this letter the managers of the Boston Theatre published a protest, in which they stated, that having suffered not only severe mortification from the disappointment experienced by the public, but heavy pecuniary loss from Kean's non-fulfilment of his engagement, they indulged a hope they would not in addition be accused of concurring in any offence to the public. Mr. Kean had, however, reduced them to the unpleasant alternative of either by silence admitting the truth of his statement regarding them, or of publicly disavowing it; they therefore stated his refusal to perform the part of Richard III. was not only without their consent, but met from them all the opposition in their power which they thought decorous and gentlemanly. This declaration was dictated by a sense of the duty they owed to the patrons of the drama; and when they added that he was not to receive any specific sum for his services, but was to share the receipts, it was evident that interest as well as duty would prevent them from concurring in his decision.

To this Kean made no reply. His assailants now attacked him with increased and undeserved bitterness, and he abandoned the resolution of again visiting Boston. In a letter addressed to the press he says—

"As I find it impossible for individual efforts to

stem the torrent of opposition with which I have to contend, and as I likewise consider it inconsistent with my feelings and character to make additional apologies, I have resolved to return to my native country, and beg leave to offer to the public my thanks for that portion of favour bestowed on me, and respectfully bid them farewell. Had I been aware of the enormity of the offence which has excited so much indignation, I certainly should not have permitted my feelings to interfere with my interest. The 'very head and front of my offending' amounts to this—an actor, honoured and patronized in his native country, and enjoying a high rank in the drama, withheld his services under the impression that they were not duly appreciated; and so much do I fear the frailty of my nature, that it is not impossible, under the same circumstances, I might be tempted to act in the same manner. I therefore think it proper to leave the theatre open to such compeers whose interest it may be to study the customs, and not offend them by my presence any longer.

"Before I left England I was apprised how powerful an agent the press was in a free country, and I was admonished to be patient under the lashes that awaited me; and at a great sacrifice of feeling I have submitted to their unparalleled severity and injustice. I was too proud to complain, and suffered in silence; but I have no hesitation in saying, that the conduct I pursued was that which every man would pursue under the same circumstances in the country where Shakespeare was born and Garrick acted.

"Again I disclaim any intention of offending; and although every natural and domestic tie, as well as the public love, await me on my own shores, it is with reluctance and regret I leave my friends in America."

When off Sandy Hook he addressed a farewell letter to the editor of the *Advocate*, begging he would impress upon the public mind the fact that he felt the highest admiration and respect for the American public. "And though," he added, "I have temporarily yielded to the torrent of hostility, which I was too proud to contend against, still on the termination of my Drury Lane engagement, I shall return again to share the favour of those friends, whom I shall ever rank foremost in my affections, in whatever clime fortune may dispose me."

Before leaving New York he expressed a wish to raise, at his own expense, a monument to George Frederick Cooke, who died in that city in September, 1812, and was buried in St. Paul's Church. Neither tablet nor tomb marked the place of his rest—a neglect Kean sought to remedy. He therefore consulted his friend Dr. Francis regarding his desire, and by his advice they waited on Bishop Hobart for permission to have Cooke's remains removed from the stranger's vault where they lay, and placed in some suitable spot in the adjoining burial-ground, over which a monument might be erected. To this the bishop, who was favourably impressed by Kean's manner, readily gave his consent, and the work was begun. One summer night, when all tumult was hushed and the world was calm, Kean and his friend set out for this city of the dead lying peaceful beneath the pale light of moon and stars. Workmen awaited them, lanterns were lighted, the heavy doors of the dark and humid vault forced open, and Kean, who exhibited a strong and morbid interest in the exhumation, descended to this charnel-house, where strangers in a strange land, homeless or nameless, found rest and peace in darkness and oblivion. The case in which the poor player had lain for over eight years was identified, and when, by Kean's request, the lid was raised, the yellow glare of lanterns fell upon a fleshless, eyeless skull, a few bones, and a handful of dust; this being all that was left of one whose soul had moved thousands to fear and pity, to hope and despair. Kean, ever susceptible to impressions, gazed with sadness at this most pitiful sight—the sternest rebuke which human vanity can know; speculated as to when his turn should come to perish in like manner; spoke words of charity towards the dead; and by way of recalling his memory in the future, as well as in recollection of this hour and scene, removed and carried away with him the bones of the fore-finger of the skeleton's right hand. Leaving the vault, a little procession of dark figures carrying a coffin in their midst silently crossed the grass-grown mounds, and lowered their burden in a new-made grave. Above this spot was placed, on the 4th of June, 1821, a pedestal supporting an urn with the following inscription—

ERECTED TO THE MEMORY

OF

George Frederick Cooke,

BY

EDMUND KEAN,

OF THE THEATRE ROYAL, DRURY LANE.

1821.

" Three kingdoms claimed his birth ;
Both hemispheres pronounce his worth."

The day on which the monument was placed in the

graveyard of St. Paul's Church terminated Kean's first visit to America. In the afternoon he repaired to this spot, and, overcome by various feelings, wept freely. "I gazed upon him," writes Dr. Francis, "with more interest than had ever before been awakened by his stage representations. I fancied—and it was not altogether fancy—that I saw a child of genius on whom the world at large bestowed its loftiest praises, while he himself was deprived of that solace which the world cannot give—the sympathies of the heart." Next day he was on his way to England.

On the 19th of July, 1821, the date on which George IV. was crowned, Kean arrived in Liverpool, from where he at once wrote to the manager of Drury Lane—

"MY DEAR ELLISTON,

"With those feelings which an Englishman can alone understand, I have touched once again my native land. I shall be at the stage-door of Drury at noon on Monday next. Do you think a few nights now would be of advantage to you? I am full of health and ambition, both of which are at your service, or they will run riot.

"EDMUND KEAN."

This note was handed to the manager by a friend of the tragedian, who suggested it would doubtless prove gratifying to Kean if his return were marked by some show of attention. Elliston, believing he wished to act on Monday evening, immediately had enormous play-bills printed and posted all over the town, respectfully informing the public that, in consequence of a letter received on Saturday from Kean, he "had the gratification of announcing that this eminent actor will re-appear as Richard III. on Monday."

Arrangements were also made to receive Kean in a manner which would gratify him. Accordingly, towards noon on Monday a procession wound its way through the streets of London, and drew up at the entrance to Drury Lane Theatre. First came six outriders in livery, followed by Elliston in his carriage drawn by four grays; next Kean in a carriage drawn by four black horses; then three members of the company drawn by four piebald ponies; and finally, a troop of horsemen brought up the rear. As the hero of the procession descended, ringing cheers were given by the crowd which had followed in his wake. This reception pleased him, and although he was surprised to find himself advertised to play that evening, and fatigued by his journey, he appeared before a densely-crowded house, that greeted him with shouts of welcome and demonstrations of joy. He had been announced to appear as Brutus on the following evening, but was obliged to request his audience to grant him a day's rest. On Wednesday he acted Shylock, on Thursday Othello, and on the following Monday Richard III., which, owing to his ill-health, was his last appearance that season.

By November he was quite recovered, and prepared to meet his old friends, the public. During the following season he appeared as Hastings in *Jane Shore*, Jaffier in *Venice Preserved*, De Montford in Joanna Baillie's tragedy of that name, Sir Pertinax Macsycophant in the *Man of the World*, Osmond in the *Castle Spectre*, and Don Felix in the *Wonder*, in none of which did he add to his success. In the summer of 1822 he went on a professional tour, and whilst in the Isle of Bute saw a charming cottage built on the banks of Loch Fad, and surrounded by wild and picturesque scenery. Of this building he desired to become the possessor, and entering into communication with its owner, Lord Bute, he immediately purchased the property. Here, with his wife and son, he settled for the autumn, busied himself with improvements he intended to make, planted a mulberry tree, and selected a spot where he declared he would make a vault for the reception of his remains.

While Drury Lane Theatre was closed Elliston had the whole interior of the building reconstructed; the parapet of the boxes being brought forward five feet, the pit made smaller, and the ceiling bodily lowered fourteen feet, whilst the great salon was lined with looking-glasses, and the pilasters painted to represent Sienna marble; the cost of the whole amounting to twenty-two thousand pounds. In September the ceremony of "striking the scaffold" took place, when Elliston bethought of giving a little dinner-party on the scaffolding; and accordingly, a dozen of his friends assembled in mid air, about five feet from the ceiling and fifty from the floor of the pit. Here on a platform that vibrated with every movement, a repast, chiefly consisting of beef-steaks, was cooked and served; wine circulated freely, and wit was exchanged.

"It is amazingly cold here," said Elliston, shivering.

"That is easily accounted for—we are near the poles," replied Beazley the architect. The heavy tread of waiters set the whole party in motion, and the manager began to feel somewhat uncomfortable, but sought to hide his nervousness under a joke. "This is at present our board," he said; "I should be very sorry if it were our lodging."

"It is your proper place," replied Wallack, one of his company. "You hold the highest situation in the theatre."

Elliston just then accidentally dropped his carving-knife, which fell between two boards, and snapping, went below.

"There—there's a blade in the pit!" he exclaimed.

"And Handel in the orchestra," added Beazley.

Elliston's health was then proposed, "and success to him in his adventurous undertaking," in reply to which the manager rose to return thanks; but at that instant a jarring sound falling on their ears, he asked what this meant. The builder replied, it was merely the labourers who were beginning to untie the cross-pole in order to strike the scaffolding.

"In that case," Elliston hastened to state, "the sooner I return thanks for the honour you have done me the better, for I now think it high time to descend." On which the party broke up.

In order to commemorate the alterations made, a brass plate was placed in the centre of the pit bearing the following inscription—

GEORGE IV. KING.

Theatre Royal, Drury Lane.

The interior of this NATIONAL THEATRE was entirely pulled down and rebuilt, in the space of fifty-eight days, and reopened on the 12th of October, 1822,

BY

ROBERT WILLIAM ELLISTON, Esq.

On the day of the opening of Drury Lane Theatre this season Mrs. Garrick died. She was dressed for attending the play on this very evening.

Whilst Kean was still enjoying the tranquillity of his new home, he received a letter from the treasurer of Drury Lane Theatre, stating that the manager had engaged Charles Young to act with him (Kean) during the coming season. Being wrathful at this unexpected intelligence, he immediately wrote the following characteristic letter—

"*Rothsay, Isle of Bute,* Oct. 28.

"ELLISTON,

"I cannot be in London till Monday the 11th of next month. Advertise me for Richard on that night.

You must forgive my being jealous of my hard-earned laurels. Young has many advantages that I have not —a commanding figure, sonorous voice, and, above all, lordly connections. I kick all such pests to the devil, for I hate a lord. I am therefore coming to meet an opposition made up of my own enemies (which, like locusts, almost darken the sun)—Mr. Young's friends, and his very great abilities—with nothing but humble genius to support me, a mere ephemeron, at the command of caprice; the same breath that nourishes the flame this day to-morrow puts it out. *Aut Cæsar aut nullus* is my text. If I become secondary in any point of view, I shrink into absolute insignificance.

".I have taken a house in Scotland for the purpose of retirement with my family at the termination of my engagements, and all I ask of you is, to let me go with my reputation undiminished. As the Covent Garden hero comes upon my ground the challenger, I have doubtless my choice of weapons; he *must* play Iago before I act Jaffier. I am told he is wonderfully great in Pierre; if so, I am beaten. This must not be; I cannot bear it. I would rather go in chains to Botany Bay. I am not ashamed to say I am afraid of the contest. Will you take the thousand pounds and dismiss me?

"Elliston, my *dear* Elliston, I *know you*. I see the deep, entangled web you have extended for me; but that Providence which has guided me through all the perils of worldly chicanery, fights for me now, and will defeat the plot, though *Coutts's Bank* flowed into the coffers of my enemy, and its suite composed of lords and auctioneers.

"Yours,

"KEAN."

On his return to Drury Lane on the 11th of November, 1822, he played Richard III.; four evenings later he acted Othello to the Iago of "a gentleman from Liverpool," and twelve nights after he repeated the same character to the Iago of Charles Young. The contest, as it was felt to be, created an excitement almost equal to that which had awaited the performance of Kean and Booth a few years previously. Kean, it was felt, would exert his strength to destroy Young's claims to rivalry; whilst the latter, it was known, would use all endeavours to excel in a combat on which so much depended. The press indeed warned Young of what might be in store for him. "We saw Junius Brutus Booth, another self-opinionated chief tragedian, try a fall (to use a wrestling term) with Kean," says the *London Magazine*. "Those who were present on that memorable occasion well know Mr. Kean can be irritated into greatness on great occasions; and if Mr. Young contests the ground with that ardent creature, he will learn a lesson which will be useful to him as long as he remains on the stage."

Young was, however, confident in his own powers, and relying on the popularity he had gained, and the support of his influential friends, entered the lists. During the first two acts he was continually applauded by a brilliant house; his precise method of delivery, cold and dignified action, never moved by a breath of passion or a flash of inspiration, being lauded by the admirers of the Kemble school; but in the third act, when Kean had gathered strength, and betrayed his fervid love and terrible fear, his maddening jealousy and black despair, Young, with his measured tones and careful gestures, was swept as it were from the minds of all present by the overwhelming grandeur of Kean's acting.

"The agony of his heart," Hazlitt finely said, speaking of this occasion, " was the fiery Moorish agony, not cramped in within an actor's or a schoolman's confines, but fierce, ungovernable, dangerous. You knew not what he would do next in the madness of his spirit—he knew not himself what he should do. Mr. Young wisely kept to his preconcerted rule, and acted by rule steadily. The fine third act dragged tediously and miserably over his tongue; and in that passage which we have always regarded as the most terrific and intense piece of dramatic writing ever accomplished—'Did Michael Cassio, when you wooed my lady, know of your love?' he was ineffective. One of the finest instantaneous actions of Kean was his clutching his black hand slowly round his head as though his brain were turning, and then writhing round and standing in dull agony with his back to the audience. What other performer would have so forgotten himself? We think Mr. Kean played more intensely on Mr. Booth's *benefit*, but then he had a motive and a cue for passion with which Mr. Young was wanting. He had to show that Mr. Booth was not of his quality. No one accuses Mr. Young of approaching him." From that evening all rivalry between Kean and Young was set at rest.

In the course of the same season Elliston announced that, "in obedience to the suggestion of men of literary eminence from the time of Addison, that the original fifth act of *King Lear* should be restored, the proprietor deems it his duty to pay deference to such opinion, and on the 10th of February Mr. Kean will conclude the character of Lear as originally written by Shakespeare." It had long been the tragedian's desire to play the part as set down by the great dramatist; for a London audience, he said, could have no notion of his power until they saw him over the dead body of Cordelia. In this estimate of himself he was not mistaken. The tragic intensity of his grief, the weird agony of his despair, the terrible pathos of his death, moved the hearts of all beholders, and dimmed their eyes with tears.

Not satisfied with the position he held at Drury Lane, Charles Young returned to Covent Garden, even as Booth had done when overwhelmed by Kean's greatness; and Macready, having quarrelled with the management of the latter theatre, was engaged by Elliston at a salary of twenty pounds a night. It was the manager's desire that Kean and Macready should play in the same pieces, but to this Kean would not listen. He "did not mind Young, but would not act with Macready," he said. What his objections were he did not state, but his reluctance certainly was not based on a fear of measuring his strength with Macready; and persevering in his resolution in spite of Elliston's entreaties, the two actors were not included in the same cast.

His fame remained undiminished, his playing drew crowds to the theatre, his name was lauded; but meanwhile, a little cloud had gathered on the horizon, which was soon to darken and ruin his life.

CHAPTER IV.

Edmund Kean and his son—A night drive—A day at Boulogne—A drama in real life—Alderman Cox and his wife—Joe Cowell's story—Evidence given at the trial—Kean's letters—Result of the action—Kean determines to face the public—A Visit from Elliston—Storms at Drury Lane—Behaviour of the press and the public—Kean resolves to visit America—Eccentricity of his conduct—His condition at this period—Meeting with J. B. Booth—Booth's eccentricities—His adventures in America—Life at the farm.

THOUGH Edmund Kean had now reached the highest point in his profession, and gained more wealth than he had ever dreamt of possessing, the realization of his ambitions by no means rendered him happy. Becoming nervous, he believed his death was at hand, continually dwelt on the instability of his success, grew uncertain in his temper, melancholy in his moods, and to banish depression, drank deeper than was his wont. It was evident some fear weighed him down, some shadow enveloped him from which he could not escape; the world which should have been fair to his eyes grew dark; oppression freighted him.

Whilst suffering from one of his unhappy moods, he returned home from the theatre one night still dressed in the costume of Richard III., the character he had just been playing—the paint still upon his cheeks, mock jewels yet upon his breast. Entering the sitting-room where his wife and son were reading, he sullenly flung himself upon a sofa, not speaking until he called for brandy. Presently Mrs. Kean, in her endeavour to soothe and interest him, talked of their son, and remarked, "Do you know he can act?"

"Indeed," he replied briefly.

"He has just been reciting some speeches to me in an excellent manner, as you will say when you've heard him."

She then asked Charles to repeat his performance, which he did, glancing apprehensively now and then at the paint-stained face and dark eyes of his father. When the lad had finished a slight pause followed, which Kean at last broke by saying, "That will do; go to bed. Good night; but remember, we will have no more acting."

Charles left the room chilled and dismayed, and as the door closed behind him Kean turned to his wife and said, "The boy might succeed as an actor; but if he tries, I will cut his throat." And jumping up he paced the room excitedly, muttering in response to Mrs. Kean's remonstrance, "I am the first and shall be the last tragedian of my name. The name shall die with me, and be buried in my coffin."

When by slow degrees his anger had subsided, his wife retired to bed, but scarce had she fallen asleep when she was roused by a noise in the adjoining room, and rising hurriedly, she inquired the cause of the disturbance, when her husband's dresser told her he was getting ready his master's clothes, as he was going out for a drive. It was then three o'clock in the morning. A hackney coach was sent for, in which Kean placed a favourite spaniel named Portia, a case of pistols, two lighted candles, and a bottle of brandy. He then entered, and bade his dresser mount the box beside the driver; when the latter inquired where he was to go, Kean replied, "To Hell." Away they drove until, arriving in the vicinity of Waterloo Place, Kean told the coachman to stop, and bidding him await his return, got out and disappeared. Minutes lengthened to hours, and hours brought day, but he failed to make his appearance, whereon the coachman drove back to the tragedian's home, from which he was yet absent.

Eccentricities such as these were not uncommon occurrences in his life. On one occasion, after he had played

Brutus, he suddenly expressed his desire to drive over to Streatham on "an experimental project," as he stated, to recover the exhaustion caused by his acting. On his way through Brixton he was attracted by a crowd around a public-house, which he immediately joined. It was principally composed of drovers, who had been drinking freely, one of whom was having a dispute with a ratcatcher, in which Kean at once took part, and offered to act as judge; on this the drover saluted him with some unfriendly words, when the tragedian seizing a pint mug, flung it in his face. The drover immediately jumped from a barrel of herrings on which he had been sitting, and rushed at his assailant, on which a free fight took place, that ended badly for Kean, who, bruised and bleeding, was put into his coach and driven home. Indeed as time passed his conduct became more reckless, his spirits more depressed, the cause of which soon become apparent to all.

In the summer of 1824 he and his wife, whilst at Boulogne on their homeward way, accidentally hearing that Mr. Grattan, the friend of their earlier days, was living with his family in the town, hastened to call on them. Kean and his wife had just returned from a second visit to Paris and Switzerland, and were now waiting for a boat to carry them to Dover. Whilst they were recounting some details of their journey to the host and hostess, an old theatrical manager named Penley, whose troupe, well-known in France and Flanders, was then playing at Boulogne, desired to see Kean, and being admitted to his presence recounted his many hardships, dwelt on his ill-luck, mentioned the poverty of his company, and finally besought Kean to act for them, offering him half the receipts of the house. The tragedian pleaded the fatigue he had suffered from having travelled the previous night as his excuse for refusing Penley; but the old man pressed him so hard, that he, who was ever easily moved by distress, consented to stay the night.

Bills were immediately printed and issued all over the town announcing the great tragedian's appearance for one night only in the character of Shylock; the prices of admission were doubled, and the theatre was densely crowded.

The receipts of the house compensated Penley for a long run of misfortune, and helped him to defy starvation for many a day to come; nor were the members of his company less grateful than he to Kean, who divided his share of the profits amongst them.

But notwithstanding the distraction caused by this incident, it was noticeable that his spirits were greatly depressed, as if some dreaded catastrophe awaited him; and when opportunity occurred, he told Grattan a trial was then pending between himself and Alderman Cox, in which the latter sued him for two thousand pounds as compensation for loss of the affection and company of his wife. On the 17th of the following January, the case was heard before Lord Chief Justice Abbott and a special jury in the Court of King's Bench. The drama, of which this action was the last scene, had begun eight years previously. At that time whilst playing Othello at the Taunton Theatre, Kean was attracted by a bright-complexioned, showily-dressed woman in a stage box; it was evident she paid great attention to his performance, for so impressed was she by its force, that towards the close of the fourth act she fainted. Considerable confusion followed, the play was interrupted, and the unconscious lady lifted across the stage, and placed in Kean's dressing-room. There, when the curtain fell the actor received her apologies for intrusion, listened to her expressions of admiration, and was introduced to her husband, Robert Albert Cox, an alderman of the city of London, twelve years her senior. In 1805 Mr. Cox, then a widower with an only son, had married her, and received as her dowry a handsome fortune. The lady was described by plaintiff's counsel as possessing "considerable mental accomplishments, and an admiration for Shakespeare and the drama;" whilst her husband's nature was, by the same authority, stated to be "tender, confiding, fond, and unsuspicious."

Delighted at making the acquaintance of the famous actor, the alderman expressed his hopes he would call upon him on his return to London, a wish seconded by Mrs. Cox, and in due course Mr. and Mrs. Kean visited them, when hospitalities were continually interchanged. Intimacy between Kean and his new friends rapidly ripened, until it became evident to Mrs. Kean a sentiment warmer than friendship existed between her husband and Mrs. Cox; when she, in the presence of that lady and her husband, declared it better all acquaintance between them should cease, after which she refused to visit their house, or receive them in hers. But this rebuff by no means altered the conduct of the confiding alderman or his charming spouse. They both entertained Kean continually, the latter generally occupying his box when he played, and visiting him in his dressing-room, now accompanied by her husband, again in company with her niece, Miss Wickstead, who was in her confidence, and frequently going there alone.

James Newman, Kean's theatrical dresser, in evidence

given at the trial, said he had known Kean refuse Mrs. Cox admission to his dressing-room, and by Kean's direction he had repeatedly declined to allow her to enter. Moreover, it frequently happened that the tender, fond, and unsuspicious husband, after Kean's performances, brought him back to his home in Wellington Street, and not only entertained him at supper, but persuaded him to remain all night beneath his hospitable roof. Joe Cowell tells a story concerning the alderman which bears upon the case. Years previously, when this excellent comedian was a member of the Drury Lane company, he saw Mr. Cox come into the principal green-room in his riding-coat, wearing very muddy boots. At this period the apartment was regarded as a drawing-room, and a rule obtained that a forfeit of a guinea should be paid by any one entering it in undress, those who were habited for the parts they played being exempt from the fine. Now the alderman's spurs catching in a lady's train, Oxberry good-humouredly reminded him of the forfeit, which by no means pleased him, but next day a note was sent by him to the theatre addressed to the gentlemen of the green-room, begging them to accept a dozen of Madeira. In return they gave him a dinner at the Freemason's Tavern on one of the days in Lent when the theatre was closed. It was noticed at this festive gathering that Kean, contrary to his usual habit, drank very little wine, and on being pressed to be more free with his glass, Cox replied, " In my official capacity I have excused Mr. Kean. The fact is, I have made a promise for him that he shall spend the evening with my wife, and if he takes too much wine, I don't know what may be the consequences." At which speech the accommodating alderman laughed right merrily. Kean withdrew early in the evening, whilst Cox remained with his hosts until three in the morning.

So familiar indeed did Kean become with the alderman and his wife, that he was, whether the former was at home or abroad, in the habit of spending nights at Wellington Street. Meanwhile, a correspondence was carried on between Mrs. Cox and the tragedian, which left no doubt concerning their relations. The lady was poetically addressed as " my heart-strings," and assured that the writer and she were created for each other; " the assimilation of disposition in all its character" proclaimed the fact, and he could, if he were not a philosopher, revile most impiously the dark fate which had given her to another. The theatre, he tells her in writing from Lynn, where he was fulfilling an engagement, " was crowded last night to excess, and the applause was as enthusiastic as it could be for the country, but Charlotte did not hear it; the neighbourhood is beautiful, the walks enchanting, but Charlotte does not partake (?) them." Then he cries out, "Fly swift, ye hours, until we meet once more."

That he was thoroughly fascinated by this woman there is no doubt, and that she, a heartless coquette, used his blind passion for her own and her husband's benefit was evident to all. The sums she received from him, whose generosity amounted to extravagance, can only be guessed from the occasional reference to money which their correspondence contained, and from evidence given. James Newman remembered handing an envelope containing notes to Miss Wickstead for Mrs. Cox one evening at the theatre; and Kean writes to her, "What money you want you shall have at three hours' notice." When in Londonderry, he tells her, "I cannot send you the money, for there are no banks here, or in any other town that I have been acting in, but write to Holton," and he encloses a note for Holton, saying he was to let her have "whatever money she may ask you for in my name."

Mrs. Cox was indeed described by the defendant's counsel as "a woman of abandoned character," who, as he chastely expressed it, "admitted the embraces of other persons beside Mr. Kean," a statement which evidence confirmed; for it appeared that one evening, some years before, on the alderman returning home somewhat earlier than was expected, and going straight to his wife's room, his attention was, by the barking of a lap-dog, attracted to a closet, opening the door of which, Sir Robert Kemyss coolly stepped out, and politely apologized for his intrusion. But this little incident in domestic life failed to have the effect of rousing the animosity of a fond and trusting husband; and it remains to be stated, as an example to his kind, it was wholly ineffectual to lessen the affection he felt for his wife.

On Kean's departure for America Mrs. Cox had volunteered to accompany him, a favour he declined. Their correspondence, however, continued, and she, during his tour, betrays an anxiety to know how much money he is making. On his return their intimacy continued, to the great distress of Mrs. Kean, who bore her wrongs with patience, and sought to save him from ruin. Continual mention is made of her from this period in his letters. "I have not heard from her lately," he writes from Scotland, "she may be on her way to me; they may follow me. We have had one dreadful instance of that. My dear love, for Heaven's sake be guarded." Later, he informs his "heart-strings" that Mrs. Kean left him yesterday for London. "If," he continues, "that had not been the case, I could not have written to you now. I am watched more closely than Bonaparte at St. Helena. She gave me a hint about meeting me at Barnet on Monday morning, but if everything should concur smoothly to bring you to St. Albans, I would take another road to London." Back again in town, the injured wife did not relax her observation. "Some evil spirit has got into our home," he states. "I cannot see what is the matter. I dare not go out alone. She says she has as much right to pay visits as me, and is determined that Charles or herself accompanies me wherever I go until I leave London;" and the day following, he informs his beloved Charlotte, "she has taken it into her head to accompany me wherever I go, and I cannot shake her off. You must guess my mortification; the eyes of Argus may be eluded, but those of a jealous wife—impossible. Even now I am on tenter-hooks. I expect the door forced open, and 'What are you writing?' the exclamation, of Susan to see if everything is comfortable, or Charles with a handful of endearment for his dear papa, all tending to the same thing—'What is he about?'" He rejoices to think the boy will soon go to school, and give him more leisure to write love-letters; but later on we find "Charles and his schoolmaster behind the scenery, and Mrs. Kean, with a large party, in front," interfering with the visits of the siren.

Occasionally the wife's vigilance was eluded. Whilst playing in Bath, in June, 1822, he writes his "darling love" a characteristic note. "I am in such a vortex of perplexities and mortifications," he says, "that I can scarce collect my thoughts sufficiently to thank you for your letter, and to tell you how much I love you. It is now, my dearest girl, I wish for you, now that I am suffering under the most painful sensations of wounded pride, my mind boiling with rage and grief; want now my own dear darling, my love, to condone with; my fevered head wants rest in the bosom of my Charlotte. Indignation, resentment, and all the passions of the furies guide my hand, while I tell you that in this infernal city, where I was a few years since the idol of the people, my endeavours are totally failing. I have not yet acted one night to the expenses; come to me, my darling, come to me, or I shall go mad. If my provincial career is followed up by this terrible sample, heaven or hell must be opened for me. I bore my elevation with philosophy; I feel I cannot long submit to the opposite. Meet me as soon as possible at Birmingham, that is, as soon as safety will permit, and believe me, I love you to distraction, and in heart I am solely yours for ever, ever, ever."

Taking Miss Wickstead with her, Mrs. Cox hastened to Birmingham, where she took up her residence at Kean's lodgings. She had left word she was going to Brighton to visit her mother, but on its being discovered she was not there, her anxious husband sent his son in search of her to Birmingham, where he knew Kean was playing. The young man found his stepmother, and returned to town with tidings of her, but this philosophic husband was not roused to indignation. "My uncle," said Miss Wickstead, on being examined in court, "never asked me or my aunt any questions about that journey." Nay, he consented to accompany his wife and Kean on an excursion taken some months subsequently.

Late one January night Kean came to the alderman's house, and after supper, suddenly proposed they should all start for Croydon, where he was to act the following evening. His carriage, which was waiting at the door, would, he said, convey them. Miss Wickstead, that she might enjoy the drive, was roused out of bed, and Kean's dresser was sent for that directions might be given him. At three o'clock they were ready to start, and as Cox stepped into the carriage, Kean in an audible voice told Newman to bring him down some money in the morning.

This romance in real life ended by Mrs. Cox becoming enamoured with a young man named Watmore, a clerk in her husband's office, while Kean's infatuation was still at its height, and he would, as he wrote, " banish every pleasure in life, shut himself up in the most dreary cavern, undergo every privation, lose even the recollection of language for want of use, if even at the end of twenty years he was sure of making her his own."

The alderman's business affairs, long in an embarrassed condition, now became desperate, and it was necessary he should have a large sum of money; therefore it happened one morning that his wife and his niece, with his consent, set out for Dover, but scarce had they departed when, on going to an unlocked cabinet in his own bed-room, what should this worthy man and trusting husband discover, but a great bundle of letters addressed by Kean to his wife, which revealed to his shocked senses the terrible injury which had been done him. For him there was but one resource left to avenge his outraged honour, and he at once decided on appealing to the law for satisfaction in the shape of two thousand pounds.

In a little while the guilty wife returned to town, but her husband, kind to the last, took lodgings for her in a house in Norfolk Street, where, strange to relate, Watmore soon took up his residence. Kean's letters, containing many extravagant expressions of affection, were read aloud at the trial, amidst the laughter of the court, and printed in almost every newspaper in London. Two points, however, in this unfortunate case redounded to his honour — he refused to put forward Mrs. Cox's letters as part of his defence, and in his own letters, " even whilst the world was a vast and gloomy dungeon" with his wife, he is firm in his determination of not abandoning her. "After my duty to my family," he writes to Mrs. Cox, "I am all in all yours for ever." The alderman did not seek a divorce or a separation from his wife, but sued for damages for the loss he sustained in her affections. The jury, having deliberated ten minutes, returned a verdict awarding him eight hundred pounds, a decision that was received with signs of surprise and disapprobation by those in court.

Seeing himself the dupe of a heartless woman and a mercenary man, the laughing-stock of the town, estranged from his family, and shunned by many friends, Kean felt the full force of the blow which had fallen on him. His pride, however, forbade him to exhibit his feelings, and in order that he might seem indifferent to the ridicule and abuse rained on him, he resolved to face the public, and by the force of his genius overcome the feelings which threatened his unpopularity. It occurred to Elliston that Kean's appearance on the stage whilst the town was still excited by the trial was an injudicious movement; but the tragedian had little fear concerning the result, and insisted on being announced to play Richard III. on the 24th of January, 1825, just a week later than the date on which the verdict of his trial had been delivered. Three days previous Sir Richard Birnie, at the request of Mr. Secretary Peel, called on Elliston, and represented the inadvisability of Kean coming forward so soon; when the manager, somewhat alarmed, immediately sought Kean at Croydon, where he then resided. Kean, he was told, was resting, but would see him, and accordingly he was shown into the presence of the tragedian, whom he found seated on a couch smoking a cigar, a glass of brandy and water close by him, whilst at the lower end of the room a fantastically-dressed dancing-girl and an acrobat were performing for his amusement. Elliston at once entered on the business of his visit, and strove to persuade him to postpone his intended appearance;

but to this Kean would not listen. He declared himself "ready for war," and stated that on the 24th instant he would meet his enemies on that ground which, by the commom assent of all England, was his own. "In the meantime," he observed, "see how quietly I am living here."

Kean's determination caused great excitement throughout the town. On the afternoon of the 24th immense crowds collected round the doors of the theatre, and by six o'clock the various streets leading to Drury Lane were completely blocked. Men and women, overcome by crushing, fainted; children who had been taken by their foolish parents were handed out over the heads of the people. On the doors being opened a tremendous rush was made, and the pit and galleries were immediately crowded; the money-takers then stated all places were filled, but fresh numbers hurrying breathlessly into the house, without hesitation betook themselves to the boxes and first circle, of which they held possession, despite the protests and threats of the door-keepers.

A deafening din of voices calling to each other from pit to circle, from boxes to gallery, shouting Kean's name with comments favourable and unfavourable, quoting notably ridiculous extracts from his letters amidst jeers and laughter, making inquiries for his heart-strings, and his little darling, filled the house. It was evident most of those present were there to enjoy excitement as well as reprove immorality, and there could be no doubt of the storm soon to ensue. The members of the orchestra took their places and began an overture, which none but themselves could hear because of the general confusion; then the curtain rose and the play began, but the actors' voices could not reach the audience. Cries of Kean, Kean, now and then rose from his partisans, which called forth a chorus of groans and hisses from his opponents; for it seemed as if the moral reputation of England was at stake, and must be vindicated by the punishment of this black sheep. Soon Kean came forward, and advanced to the centre of the stage, as was his custom on entering as Richard. Then up rose the pit in its strength; yells, hootings, cries mingled with cheers, and the clapping of hands, a wild, mad, deafening tumult in all, swelling every instant, burst upon him, hearing which he stood still, scared and bewildered by the fierceness of the tempest his presence had evoked. Recovering himself quickly he bowed, but if he expected his audience would permit him to speak he was grievously disappointed. The fury, if possible, increased, and assured he would not be heard, he began his part, the noise completely drowning his voice, so that the scene was performed in dumb-show.

Meanwhile the two factions in the pit came to blows, and the attention of the house was occasionally turned from the stage to watch various combatants; whilst some occupants of the boxes and circle who objected to settle their disputes in a rough and ready manner, presented each other with cards, as polite preliminaries to exchanging shots. To vary the monotony of the proceedings some young men began a chorus from *Der Freischutz*, which had the effect of adding to the general uproar. In the course of the first act, the din becoming intolerable to Kean, he advanced to the front of the stage, and removed his hat to show he was anxious to address the house, but this action merely served to heighten the dire confusion. "Off! off!" cried his opponents, "a public insult!" To which his partisans replied, "Kean for ever! turn out the geese." Having watched with kindling eyes the crowd, which a little while before had cheered him to the echo, now deride and insult him, he resolutely put on his hat and continued the tragedy. But once again he made a similar appeal to be heard, with no better result. His calmness and firmness exasperated his enemies, and no offensive name, no scandalous epithet, or painful allusion was spared him; nay, oranges and orange-peel were freely flung at him by some violent champions of virtue, and on one occasion whilst continuing his part he quietly unsheathed his sword, and removed from the boards some peel which had alighted near him. To the end he went through his part; "no token," as the *Morning Post* remarked with indignation and regret, "of an abashed spirit being discernible in his looks or gestures throughout." When the curtain fell Kean and Elliston were loudly called for, but neither appeared, and the audience, being hoarse and weary, quietly witnessed the succeeding farce.

Undaunted by this reception Kean again appeared before the public four days later in the character of Othello. On the previous occasion the receipts of the house amounted to seven hundred and twenty pounds; but on this evening the audience was not so great, though the excitement was not less. Before the play began a large placard bearing the words, "Kean for ever!" was lowered from the gallery, and proved a signal for an outburst of groans and hisses, taunts and jeers, as likewise for the production of other posters from various parts of the house on which were written, "No cant!" "Bravo, Kean!" "Hear his apologies." Elliston was then called for, but coming forward was not allowed a hearing, on which he retired, and the tragedy began. During the first scene a man in one of the boxes created much attention by his violent abuse of Kean, learning which the tragedian's friends in the pit singled him out as a fitting object for their wrath, and pelted him with oranges until he made a hasty retreat. As the act continued another individual, mounting on the benches in the pit, shouted out his belief that the audience of a theatre did not constitute a fitting tribunal to decide upon private affairs; and was answered that Kean had shown contempt for public opinion by appearing so soon after his trial. Three cheers were called for and given for Kean, followed by a storm of hisses, when it was suggested that "the alderman's geese" should be driven home. A general fight then ensued.

The while the performance was continued, though not a single speech or line was heard. It was succeeded by "an extraordinary popular new pantomime," the first scenes of which were interrupted by calls for Elliston, in response to which he appeared, and, somewhat to his surprise, silence was granted him. He stated that in July last he had engaged Kean to play for twenty nights, at a salary of fifty pounds a night.

At that time there was no belief the question which had lately occupied the public mind would be brought before the courts. The engagement was to begin on the 16th of January, and end on the 16th of March, and this being announced before the trial took place, Elliston would not have the tragedian's name taken from the bills. He would not use a harsh word by stating his theatre had enemies, but he would solemnly declare that neither his own power nor any influence he possessed was used to create an influence in Kean's favour. He concluded by requesting the house to hear Kean, and retiring for a second, reappeared with him. The great actor was greeted with cheers and hisses, but after a few seconds was permitted to speak. "If it is supposed," he said, "by those whom I address, that I stand before you for the purpose of explaining or justifying my private conduct, I must beg leave to state that they will be disappointed, for I am quite unable to do so. I stand before you, ladies and gentlemen, as the representative of Shakespeare's heroes, and by the public voice I must stand or fall. My private conduct has been investigated before a legal tribunal, and decency forbade my publishing letters and giving evidence that would inculpate others, though such a course would in a great degree have exculpated me.

I will not submit to be trampled upon by a hostile press; but if the public is of opinion that my conduct merits exclusion from the stage, I am ready to bow to its decision, and take my farewell."

His last words were received with shouts of "No, no; Kean for ever!" and the audience, seeming more pacified, left the house soon after. Three nights later he made his appearance as Sir Giles Overreach before a crowded assembly, the greater part of which seemed favourably disposed towards him. Peace was not, however, the order of the night, for the same bustle and clamour as reigned on former evenings was continued. When the curtain rose Kean was loudly called for, and on his coming forward was received with cheers and groans. A great part of the pit then rose and demanded the expulsion of those who had come there to persecute him, on which a general scrimmage took place, and was continued from time to time throughout the first and second acts; occasionally oranges were flung at Kean, who, it was evident, felt deeply wounded by this treatment, for more than once his countenance changed, and exhibited strong traces of emotion. When the curtain fell he was called forward, and obeying the summons of those who were curious to hear him, said, "I have made as fair concession to a British audience as a British actor ought. I hope, for the honour of my country, that I shall be permitted to perform for the remainder of twenty nights, after which I shall take my leave for ever. I hope also, for the honour of my country, that news of this persecution will never reach foreign annals."

When, four nights later, he played Macbeth, his assailants were much weaker in force, and the tragedy suffered but few interruptions; and at the conclusion he was called for, but it was stated he had left the house. From this time forward the feeling against him became less and less violent, until it eventually subsided. The feud had been to a great degree animated and strengthened by the press; references to his private life had been mixed with criticisms on his acting, and various speeches of the characters he represented were turned to personal application. In this way the *Morning Post* erred daily, but the *Times*, as a champion of purity, visited him with the blackest vials of its wrath. Kean's partisans were described by this organ as Jews, prize-fighters, and bullies, and generally referred to as vermin; it doubted if any Englishwoman of character could, "after the filthy exposure of Mr. Kean," be ever brought to visit a theatre in which he played; nay, this most chaste monitor of private morality expressed its wonder as to who the actresses were, or where they came from, whom Elliston "brought forward on the stage to be fawned upon and caressed by this obscene mimic." Is it not shocking, asks the virtuous press, "that women should be forced to undergo this process with such a wretch for want of bread?"

In a few months the world had forgotten the venomous imbecility of the *Times*, but it rankled in Kean's breast. The faithlessness of the woman for whom he had risked so much, the publicity given to his offence, the acrimony of those who had once been his heartiest admirers, the estrangement of his family, were afflictions that for a while almost disturbed the reason of one who had inherited a taint of madness. In March his engagement at Drury Lane ended, and it being understood that these were his farewell performances, crowds flocked to the theatre. On the last night, at the conclusion of the play, he was eagerly called for, and on coming forward, the demonstration in his favour for awhile rendered him unable to speak. He was much affected, and after some time said it might readily be understood how powerful was the gratification which prevented him from expressing his feelings. "I have," he continued, "been able to overcome one of the most powerful and most malignant attacks to which a professional man has ever been subjected." (Cries of "The rascally *Times*.") "Without alluding to past circumstances, I consider it a base plan for my destruction; and under the influence of your displeasure, which my powerful enemies endeavoured to augment, I must have sank, had not the public protected me. My gratitude is indelible, and my endeavours to merit your favours shall be unceasing."

Sick at heart from all that had happened, he now decided on making his home in America; and before starting for that country he resolved to give farewell performances in the chief provincial towns of Great Britain; but almost everywhere he encountered bitter hostility. On the announcement being made in the Edinburgh theatre of his approaching visit to that city, it was received with groans and hisses, and other "expressions of disgust and indignation;" and on silence being obtained, a red-haired Pharisee in one of the boxes rose up and stated, he would withdraw his patronage from the theatre, that no member of his family should ever again be seen within its walls, and that he should exert whatever influence he possessed in dissuading his friends from supporting a place of amusement where so little regard was paid to morality.

Under this continued persecution Kean's brain

seemed to give way; continually he mixed the words of the character he represented with an account of his private affairs; occasionally in playing tragic parts he turned somersaults and threw handsprings, saying by way of explanation, "I may as well practise, for I suppose I must come back to this;" and when he failed to perform such feats to his satisfaction, he would sadly exclaim, "I could do these things a few years ago, but I am too old and too fat now." Whilst playing at Cheltenham the editor of a journal in that town made some severe remarks concerning the late trial, and the night after reading these comments Kean, whilst acting Sylvester Daggerwood, kept a horsewhip in his hand with which he tapped his legs from time to time, and turning to the audience said, "I keep this little instrument to punish cheating aldermen and lying editors." On another occasion, whilst performing Sir Giles Overreach to a thin house at Birmingham, on an allusion being made to the marriage of his daughter, he suddenly turned to the stage-suitor and said, "Take her, sir, and the Birmingham audience into the bargain."

Later on at Greenock his reception was so hostile, that before the tragedy of *Richard III.*, in which he was playing, had finished, he suddenly left the theatre, and, dressed as the crook-backed king, went down to the harbour, got on board a yacht, and sailed for Bute, where he remained some days. Manchester, where he next appeared, welcomed him enthusiastically, and Dublin, with whose citizens he had ever been a favourite, received him with the heartiest cordiality, remembering that in the days of his prosperity he had given the receipts of a London benefit to relieve the famine-stricken Irish people. In June he was back in town, playing, as he believed, to a London audience for the last time. He was coldly received, but met with no hostility; and the evening of the 20th of July, 1825, when he concluded this series of performances, was not marked by any demonstration.

His mental and physical condition at this period is recorded by Grattan, who declares Kean never recovered from the " tumult of suffering which then assailed him." A few days before he left town on his way to America this friend called upon him. " I never saw a man so changed," he writes, " he had all the air of desperation about him. He looked bloated with rage and brandy; his nose was red, his cheeks blotched, his eyes bloodshot; I really pitied him. He had lodgings in Regent Street, but I believe very few of his former friends of any respectability now noticed him. The day I saw him he sat down to the piano, notwithstanding the agitated state of his mind, and sang for me *Lord Ullin's Daughter*, with a depth and power and sweetness that quite electrified me. I had not heard him sing for many years; his improvement was almost incredible; his accompaniment was also far superior to his former style of playing. I could not repress a deep sentiment of sorrow at the wreck he presented of genius, fame, and wealth. At this period I believe he had not one hundred pounds left of the many thousands he had received. His mind seemed shattered; he was an outcast on the world. He left England a few days afterwards, and I never dreamt of seeing him again."

On leaving London, he proceeded to Liverpool, from where he was to sail for America, and where he met Junius Brutus Booth, who had been in the States for the past four years, and was now paying a visit to England. Booth, in writing to his father, mentions the encounter with his old rival. "Kean sails the day after to-morrow by the *Silas Richards* for New York," he says. "Strange that he should meet me here—he ready to embark, and to that very country I have just left. He has been quite ill, and looks wretched. I passed an hour with him last night at his quarters, and reconciled our ancient misunderstanding. The vessel he goes in to New York will most probably be the conveyance for this letter. I really wish he may meet with success. He has been all along a victim to sharpers and flatterers, who buoyed him up with the notion of omnipotence, which now he awakens from, and perceives the hollowness of those on whom he most relied."

The while Kean had experienced triumphs and humiliations, Booth had passed through many adventures. Whilst in Liverpool early in the year 1821, the latter actor had, in a violent fit of jealousy, assaulted a tight-rope dancer known as Il Diavolo Antonio. To avoid the consequences of his action, he fled from England, accompanied by his wife, and sailed for the West Indies. The vessel in which he embarked stayed at the island of Madeira, and here he changed his mind, for instead of continuing his journey as he had originally intended, he took passage in a schooner bound for Norfolk, Virginia, where he arrived in the month of August, 1821.

By reason of his sudden departure from England, his intention of visiting the States had not been heralded in the usual manner, and he carried with him no letters of introduction. Accordingly, when a small-sized, pale-faced young man waited on Gilferet, manager of the Richmond Theatre, gave his name as Junius Brutus Booth, and declared his wish to perform,

Gilferet felt inclined to believe him an impostor desirous of humbugging the Yankees. The little man was, however, positive regarding his identity, and the manager engaged him for one night, with a conditional extension of engagement providing he proved successful. He therefore made his first appearance in the United States in the Richmond Theatre, playing on that occasion Richard III.

Gilferet's doubts were shared by others, for Richard Russell, manager of the Petersburg Theatre, hearing that Junius Brutus Booth was announced to play at Richmond, came at once to the latter city, that he might see who was the trickster assuming the name of the tragedian familiar to Drury Lane and Covent Garden. He remained to witness his performance, when he immediately concluded the little man was veritably Junius Brutus Booth, and asked him to play one night at Petersburg before he began a further engagement now offered him by Gilferet. And Booth consenting, Richard Russell returned to his theatre, and advertised his appearance. On the morning of the day he was to perform a rehearsal was called, but the English actor was absent; the manager, however, made his company go through their parts, saying that Booth could afterwards rehearse his scenes with them.

"I think they had reached the fourth act of the tragedy," says a player who was present, "and I was sauntering near the head of the stairs that led up to the stage, when a small man, that I took to be a well-grown boy of about sixteen years of age, came running up the stairs, wearing a roundabout jacket and a cheap straw hat, both covered with dust, and inquired for the stage manager. I pointed across the stage to Mr. Russell, who at that moment had observed the person with whom I was conversing, and hurried towards us, and cordially grasping the hand of the strange man, said, 'Ah, Mr. Booth, I am glad you have arrived; we were fearful something serious had happened to you.' I don't think any man was ever more astonished than I was just then on beholding this meeting. Is it possible this can be the great Mr. Booth, that Mr. Russell says is 'undoubtedly the best actor living?' and I began to think Russell was trying to put off some joke upon us all. I observed, however, that when the small man came upon the stage to rehearse his scenes he was quite at home, and showed a knowledge of the business of the character that a mere novice or pretender could not have acquired. He ran through the rehearsal very carelessly, gave very few special or peculiar directions, tried the combat of the last act over twice, and said, 'That will do,' and the rehearsal was over. He then told Mr. Russell that he had been a few minutes too late for the stage-coach, that left Richmond early in the morning, and that he soon after started on foot, and had walked all the way, twenty-five miles; that his wardrobe had been sent to the stage-office before he was up, had been taken by the coach, and he supposed was ready in the city for the proper claimant."

At night the good people of Petersburg assembled in numbers to see him, for "the first appearance of the great tragedian, Junius Brutus Booth, from the London Theatres Covent Garden and Drury Lane," had been announced in great letters all over the town. The members of the company were likewise anxious to behold one of whom they had heard much, and when not required upon the stage, gathered in groups at the wings to watch him. As the curtain rose he went forward and was warmly greeted. According to his custom, he took no notice of the demonstration, but began his part, and continued it with a placidness and seeming indifference that created general disappointment. The second act was gone through in a like manner, Booth intending in this way to heighten the force and passion he displayed in the following acts. The house became cold and careless, the company sceptical of his powers. "What do you think of him?" an old actor named Benton asked of a fellow player named Ludlow. "Why I think, as I thought before, that he is an impostor," replied the latter. "And what is your opinion of him?" "Why," answered Benton, "if the remainder of his Richard should prove like the beginning, I have never yet, I suppose, seen the character played, for it is unlike any I ever saw; it may be very good, but I don't fancy it." But the tragedian merely bided his time until opportunity was given him for the display of his powers, and when the curtain fell such applause burst from audience and actors as had never been heard in that theatre before.

He returned to Richmond, and there played a round of his favourite characters, amongst them being Sir Edward Mortimer in *The Iron Chest*, in which he usually won great applause. Booth was particularly careful about the stage business in rehearsing the scene where Wilford, his secretary, one day discovering the key in the iron chest, that is in some way connected with the gloom and mystery surrounding Sir Edward, and allowing his curiosity to overcome his scruples, lifts the lid, when he is surprised by his patron. His instructions to the young actor, James Murdock, who played the part of Wilford, were that he was, on perceiving the key, to deliberately survey the room, and satisfy himself that it was tenantless; then advancing to the chest, to go down on one knee before it, placing his left hand on the lid, and gently raising it, hold it back whilst he placed his right hand amongst the papers it contained, turning them as if seeking something hidden beneath. He was to take no heed of Sir Edward's stealthy advance, no matter how long the suspense might last, until he felt a hand upon his shoulder; then he was to turn abruptly, let the lid fall with a slam, and remain upon his knee, until a pressure of Sir Edward's hand summoned him to rise and stand before him.

On the evening of the performance young Murdock, knowing himself to be imperfect in his lines, which at a brief notice he had striven to commit to memory, felt extremely nervous. However, he managed to get through the play until the scene he had carefully rehearsed was at hand. "At length," he said, "I found myself in the presence of the mysterious chest. I was almost breathless with excitement and from anxiety, consequent on my strong desire to execute Mr. Booth's orders to the very letter. I had proceeded so far as to open the chest, and stooping over the papers, awaited trembling on my knee the appointed signal for action. The time seemed an eternity, but it came at last. The heavy hand fell on my shoulder. I turned, and there, with the pistol held to my head, stood Booth, glaring like an infuriated demon. Then for the first time I comprehended the reality of acting. The fury of that passion-flamed face and the magnetism of the rigid clutch upon my arm paralyzed my muscles, while the scintillating gleam of the terrible eyes, like the green and red flashes of an enraged serpent, fascinated and fixed me spell-bound to the spot. A sudden revulsion of feeling caused me to spring from my knees, but bewildered with fright, and a choking sensation of undefined dread, I fell heavily to the stage, tripping Mr. Booth, who still clutched my shoulder. I brought him down with me, and for a moment we lay prostrate. But suddenly recovering himself he sprang to his feet, with almost superhuman strength dragging me up, as I clung to his arm in terror. Shaking himself free of my grasp, I sank down again stunned and helpless. I was aroused to consciousness, however, by a voice calling on me in suppressed accents to rise, and then became aware that Mr. Booth was kneeling by my side. He helped me to my feet, whispering in my ear a few encouraging words, and then dexterously managed, in spite of the accident, and my total inability to speak, to continue the scene to its close. Thus was I, an unfortunate tyro, saved from disgrace by the coolness and kindness of one who had every reason to be moved by a very different state of mind; for it was evident that, but for the actor's readiness and skill in improvising the business of the stage, one of the most important and interesting scenes of the play would have proved a mortifying failure. The kindness of the act was its own reward, for the audience never evinced the slightest indication of the presence of a disturbing element, but, on the contrary, gave evidence of their satisfaction by applause at this critical moment to which I have alluded."

Having finished his engagement at Richmond, Booth played at Petersburg, and then went to New Orleans. When he had performed some nights with great success, a deputation of Frenchmen called on the manager of the theatre, and asked to be introduced to Booth, they being anxious to know if he could perform in some play of which they had more knowledge than those in which he had already appeared. Booth, feeling gratified by their desire, told them he had once played Orestes in an English translation of Racine's *Andromaque*, called *The Distressed Mother;* and if they allowed him a few days to study the part, he would act it for them. On this they expressed their gratitude and withdrew. A week later the tragedy was produced, when the theatre was crowded by French people, who understood little of the English language, but being familiar with Racine, they were enabled to follow the play, and, delighted with Booth's acting, cried out, "Talma! Talma! Talma!" Finally, when at the end of the last act he died in a raving fit of madness, their enthusiasm knew no bounds.

He made his first appearance in New York at the Park Theatre on the 5th of October, 1821, and was highly successful; he then played in the principal cities of the United States, and became one of the most popular actors that ever visited that country. By degrees the inconsistencies and eccentricities of his character became developed. Well-educated, deeply read, and refined, he frequently choose as his associates the dissipated, worthless, and ignorant; without pledging himself to any belief, he revered faith in others, and in the midst of his revelries would turn to read a chapter from the Bible with a solemnity that never failed to impress his hearers. He delighted indeed in studying religions, frequenting synagogues, and discoursing with the Rabbis, visited Catholic churches, held theological discussions with priests, and resorted to a sailor's Bethel, or floating chapel, where he knelt as one amongst the humble congregation. His respect for houses of worship was such that he never passed one without removing his hat. Not only did he read the scriptures, but likewise the Talmud and the Koran; and certain days were religiously observed by him as sacred to colour, ore, metals, &c. One of his children—whom he originally intended to call Ayesha, after Mahomet's first wife—was finally named, in accordance with the instructions he wrote to his wife, " Asia, in remembrance of that country where God first walked with man, and Frigga, because she came to us on Friday, which day is consecrated to the Northern Venus." If he were not professedly a Christian, he at least performed actions from which most of those calling themselves Christians would shrink. One day when a miserable-looking sailor came to his door to beg for bread, he not only welcomed him beneath his roof, and set food before him, but finding the man suffered from a wounded leg, Booth went down on his knees, and with great tenderness washed and bandaged the limb. And once, in passing through Louisville jail, a famous horse-stealer named Fontaine, *alias* Lovett, was pointed out to him. The man's trial had not yet taken place, and Booth was told he had no counsel; but though assured his case was hopeless, the actor sent him a lawyer, and defrayed the expenses of his defence. In gratitude Fontaine willed him his skull, desiring " that it should be given after his execution to the actor Booth, with the request that he would use it on the stage in *Hamlet*, and think when he held it in his hands of the gratitude his kindness had awakened."

In due time the skull was sent to Booth's residence whilst he was absent, but presently Mrs. Booth, regarding it with nervous horror, sent it back to the medical man who had been instructed to prepare it for the tragedian. The doctor retained the skull, and long years afterwards gave it to Edwin Booth, who used it in the grave-yard scene in *Hamlet*, but eventually had it buried.

At all times Booth strove to identify himself with the characters he was about to represent. If the part he was to play in the evening was Shylock, all that day he was a Jew, and when it was possible passed hours with the children of Israel, discussing Hebrew history with them, and insisting, as his son narrates, that though he was of Welsh descent, his nation was of Hebraic origin. Again, when about to play Othello, he was wont to wear a crescent pin in his scarf, and "disregarding the fact that Shakespeare's Moor was a Christian, would mumble maxims of the Koran." This trait continued through his life, and towards the close of his career a notable instance of it occurred. When playing Brutus to the Titus of his son in Richmond, he had arrived at the scene where the Roman consul condemns Titus to an ignominious death; his countenance showed the agony he endured, tears streamed down his cheeks, and the audience felt the spell of his power, when suddenly silence was broken by the remark of a drunken man in the gallery. Booth raised his eyes in the direction of the disturber, and in the same tones as he had last spoken said, " Beware, I am the headsman; I am the executioner." The profound stillness of the house marked the force of his words, and added to the solemnity of the scene. Occasionally his eccentricities were heightened by drink, a glass of wine, a little brandy, or a bottle of porter, his favourite drink, being sufficient to excite his sensitive brain. Times there were, however, when he wholly abstained from intoxicating drinks.

Though managers had reason to feel grateful to him as an attraction which never failed to fill their theatres, yet his habit of disappearing in the middle of an engagement without word or warning, when not in the humour to play, sometimes placed them in serious difficulties. Once when advertised to begin a series of performances on the first of April, it occurred to him it would be excellent fun to make April fools of the audience. Therefore on the evening of that day he went into the country. The crowd which awaited Booth, supposing a trick had been played on them, because the manager was anxious to fill his house, were thoroughly indignant with him; but when he came forward and declared the fault lay with the absent tragedian, and said Booth should never set his foot upon that stage again so long as he had command over it, they hissed the latter statement, and remained away from the theatre until Booth's return, which was hailed with enthusiasm.

On another occasion, when Wemyss the manager asked him to play Richelieu for his benefit, Booth declined, saying, "No, sir, no, the cardinal was tall and gaunt, I cannot look him. Announce me for Jerry Sneak or John Lump, but not for Richelieu." Wemyss persisted, and Booth consented to study the part, but on the night of its performance the Cardinal during the first act halted in his lines, hesitated, and paused, when his Eminence lightly tripped over to Father Joseph, and seizing him in his arms, waltzed with him round the stage, to the amazement of the house and the horror of the manager, who had the curtain dropped on this mad prank. Booth then disappeared, and was not seen by his friends for some days.

During an engagement at the Providence Theatre, he failed to make his appearance one evening on which he was announced to play. The house was crowded, and the unhappy manager set off in search of the eccentric tragedian. Going first to the hotel, where Booth's conduct had been a source of wonder and amusement to the proprietor and his servants, the manager and one of the clerks of the inn went to the actor's bed-room, but found the door locked; they then called aloud, but received no answer. Thinking he might have fallen asleep, the clerk climbed upon the roof of an adjacent piazza, and peered through the window, but the room was apparently empty. The corridors and adjoining apartments were searched in vain, and the anxious manager was about to continue his inquiries elsewhere, when the clerk again scaled the piazza, entered the room by the window, and looking under the bed, met the calm and sober gaze of the missing tragedian. Being discovered, he consented to proceed to the theatre, and relying on his promise, the manager hastened back to announce his coming. Booth followed him leisurely, interrupting every second person he met to inquire his way, though the route was perfectly well known to him. When at last he came upon the stage, he was received with the heartiest greetings by those whose patience he had severely tested.

Though he earned both fame and fortune by his talents, he contemplated, and frequently spoke of, "retiring into private life, and keeping a lighthouse;" and so much in earnest was he concerning this scheme, that he consulted Mr. Blunt, collector of customs, about a vacancy for the post of keeper which occurred in 1822 at Cape Halteras lighthouse, and entered with him into the question of salary and the circumstances of the office. Fortunately, he did not obtain the keepership; but in this year he purchased a farm in Harford county, Maryland, lying about twenty-five miles from Baltimore, and at an equal distance of three miles from the hamlets of Belair, Hickory, and Churchville. The farm was a clearing in a dense woodland, merging into a great forest, which on moonlight nights echoed with the ringing cries of hunters, and the deep baying of dogs in chase of opossums. The log-cabin which Booth erected here consisted of four rooms, beside the loft and the kitchen, with its enormous chimney, within whose ample space the actor, his wife, and young children, seated round a wood-fire, spent many a winter's eve. Without, the building was plastered and whitewashed, its square window-frames and door being painted red, forming a quaint and picturesque habitation, surrounded by oak, walnut, beach, and tulip trees. Not far removed was a spring bubbling up beneath thick brambles, deliciously cool at all seasons; and presently barns, stables, and a dairy were built, an orchard and vineyard planted, and habitations constructed for the negroes who worked in the fields. The rough old coach-road passing the farm was deeply shaded in summer time by massive boughs arching themselves overhead; and along this route the post-boy rode once a week, his horses' hoofs clattering with pleasant sound, his horn echoing wild notes through the forest as signal that he had tossed across the wall the welcome letter-bag, bringing news of that world which the great forest trees seemed to shut out from the dwellers in this Arcadian home.

The furniture of the cabin was plain and rough. It consisted, as Mrs. Clarke, the tragedian's daughter, who gives a pleasant picture of her early surroundings, tells us, "of a corner cupboard filled with quaint china, a narrow looking-glass with the upper half bearing a picture of the sun and moon, human faces representing each; tall brass andirons, a high brass fender, and a spinning-wheel; for it was the farmer's pride that all his blankets and woollen goods came from the backs of his own sheep, and were spun at home. An old Herbalist hung by the side of the amusing and instructive almanack on the wall; an ink-horn and a bunch of quills, together with little bags of seed and other necessary small articles, were ranged on little hooks round the looking-glass. The round Dutch oven that baked the wholesome bread, and the immense heavy pewter platters from which the simple meals were eaten, and which served in later years as covers to the milk crocks in the dairy; also the wonderful cradle-baskets for the babies, and many smaller wicker baskets of odd shapes, would now be readily secured as curiosities. Basket-weaving in the long winter evenings was the favourite occupation of old Joe— young Joe then, a faithful, trusted slave to an indulgent master."

The use of flesh food was strictly forbidden in the household, and animal life on the farm was held sacred; even the black snake, the destructive night owls, and the opossums were spared. In one of the letters written home whilst he was absent filling an engagement, Booth writes, " Tell Junius not to go opossum hunting, or setting rabbit-traps, but to let the poor devils live. Cruelty is the offspring of idleness of mind and beastly ignorance, and in children should be repressed and not encouraged, as is too often the case, by unthinking beings who surround them. A thief who takes property from another has it in his power, should he repent, to make a restoration; but the robber of life never can give back what he has wantonly and sacrilegiously taken from beings perhaps innocent, and equally capable of enjoying pleasure or suffering torture with himself. The ideas of Pythagoras I have adopted; and as respects our accountability to animals hereafter, nothing that man can preach can make me believe to the contrary. 'Every death its own avenger breeds.'"

To this home in the woods Booth retreated when not fulfilling engagements at the theatre, obtaining a needed relief in its quiet from the excitement of his life as a player. It was always with reluctance he left the farm for the noise of cities. When about to play at Baltimore, he dressed in the garb of a labourer, and usually brought to market a cart filled with vegetables, or a waggon-load of hay, by which he stood until it was time for him to visit the playhouse, and rehearse the part in which he would delight a great audience that evening. And on market nights he would join the rustics at the villages close to his home, drink with them in the taverns, and presently electrify them with a speech from *Othello,* or a soliloquy from *Hamlet.* In the autumn of 1825 he came to England, and returned to America in the spring of 1827.

CHAPTER V.

An eventful year for Edmund Kean—Before a New York audience—Behaviour of the house—An appeal to the public—Excitement at Boston—Riot in the theatre—A stormy night—Kean makes his escape—Conduct of the mob—Back in New York— Phases of insanity—Playing at Philadelphia—Visit to Charleston — A wreck of his former self— At Quebec—Amongst the Indians—Made an Indian chief—Alanienouidet on his throne—Reception of Dr. Francis—Farewell to America.

ON the 14th of November, 1825, a dark and eventful year in his life, Edmund Kean appeared as Richard III. at the Park Theatre, New York. His arrival had created a sensation in the city, and on this evening the theatre was densely thronged. When the curtain rose calls for Kean were general and vigorous, and on his coming forward a storm of groans and cheers filled the house. Walking to the centre of the stage, he bowed, folded his arms, and waited until opportunity was given him to speak; but the contending shouts of his friends and hootings of his enemies prevented his intention, and after some ten minutes spent in watching the scene he retired. Simpson the manager then appeared, and having obtained silence, requested the house would hear Kean. It was not, he said, the practise of Americans to condemn unheard, and he trusted what Kean had to say would give satisfaction.

Once more the tragedian came forward, but the hooting and cheering breaking out with renewed force, hindered him from addressing his audience, and bowing, he began the opening soliloquy of *Richard III.* The din continuing rendered the actors inaudible. References were shouted regarding Mrs. Cox and the Alderman, not quite in the spirit of decency; Kean was called many opprobrious names, and oranges were freely flung at him, one of which struck him in the breast. At this he paused, picked up the fruit, and displaying it to the audience, flung it behind the scenes with a smile of disdain. At this action the house became indignant, his friends considering it an insult, his enemies roused by his expression of contempt; so that the contention rising to fury, Hilson, a member of the orchestra, being alarmed for the safety of his wife, who played Lady Anne, jumped on the stage and led her away. This interruption of the scene added to the confusion, which was not subdued when the lady was brought back by the manager, and not one word of the tragedy from the first act to the last was heard.

Next morning Kean addressed a letter to the *New York Advocate*, in which he said, it was with feelings such as might prove heart-rending to his friends, and over which his enemies might triumph, that he appealed to a country famed for hospitality to the stranger and for mercy to the conquered. Whatever his offences were, he disclaimed any intention of disrespect to the inhabitants of New York. He could not remember an act or thought that did not prompt him to an unfeigned acknowledgment of their favours as a public, and profound admiration of their private worth. "That I have committed an error," he continues, referring to the unpleasantness which occurred at Boston during his previous visit, "appears too evident from the all-decisive voice of the public; but surely it is but justice to the delinquent (whatever may be his enormities), to be allowed to make reparation where the offences were committed. My misunderstandings took place in Boston; to Boston I shall assuredly go to apologize for my indiscretions. I visit this country now under different feelings and auspices than on a former occasion. Then I was an ambitious man, and the proud representative of Shakespeare's heroes; now the spark of ambition is extinct, and I merely ask a shelter in which to close my professional and mortal career. I give the weapon into the hands of my enemies; if they are brave, they will not turn it against the defenceless."

This abject and pathetic appeal was supplemented by an editorial remark, that offended virtue could best testify its indignation by absenting itself from the theatre, instead of converting a place of amusement to a battle-ground for contending obscenity and riot. A couple of evenings later he played Othello, when nothing could exceed the excitement of the public. When, after a considerable delay, the curtain rose, applause and hisses again filled the theatre, but the latter were in the minority. Presently Kean's supporters exhibited a poster begging his friends to be silent, when, they complying, the weakness of his enemies was discovered. By degrees signs of animosity grew less and less, until in the third act the tragedian's magnificent playing silenced all opposition, and he was heard with attention and delight. At the fall of the curtain a storm of unanimous applause arose, and he was loudly called for by an audience anxious to make some reparation for its past behaviour. Coming forward, he returned thanks for the favour granted him that evening; he stated that for his past conduct he could but express bitter regret; he had suffered enough during the last few months to atone for the blackest in the whole catalogue of crimes; and concluded by hoping Lethe's stream might be permitted to pass over his faults for ever. "The pith of the matter," says the *Albion*, referring to this speech, "the pathos and manner of its delivery, and the eloquence of appeal were powerful. The guilty offender stood before us all with the mental endowments which nature had lavished upon him, and which he seemed to deposit at the feet of the audience as a ransom for their lost favour. What a victory did genius gain over prejudice, and what a mass of anger and resentment was sacrificed on its glorious shrine." From this night forward his performances at New York were interrupted only by applause.

Having finished his engagement he went to Albany, where he was received with welcome, and then proceeded to Boston, where a far different experience awaited him. The day before his appearance in that city he addressed a letter to the public, which was inserted in the leading journals. In this he begged to inform the citizens of Boston of his arrival, confident that liberality and forbearance would gain the ascendance over prejudice and cruelty. "That I have erred," he concluded,

"I acknowledge; that I have suffered for my errors and indiscretion, my loss of fame and fortune is but too melancholy an illustration."

This epistle had the effect of irritating rather than soothing those to whom it was addressed. A hostile press tortured the fact of his not playing before a scanty audience during his first visit to their city into a gross insult, and called upon the chivalry of the people to avenge the wrongs he had heaped upon their country; whilst the incidents of his life bearing on his recent trial were repeated and magnified, until he was painted as a monster of iniquity. A general fever of excitement prevailed, and it was generally whispered that Kean would not be allowed to play. His first appearance had been announced for December 21st, 1825. Early in the day a crowd assembled round the theatre, and during the afternoon a scene of confusion and uproar ensued which promised a stormy evening. All tickets had been sold the previous day, so that when at last the doors were opened the rush was terrific, and some of those on the outer edge of the crowd, in their desperate determination to gain admittance, mounted on the shoulders and literally travelled over the heads of the mob. In a space that might be counted by seconds the theatre was densely packed by men—women having wisely absented themselves. Before the curtain drew up an actor came forward and shouted some sentences, but the uproar being great, it was impossible for him to be heard; it was evident, however, he wished to express Kean's desire to address the house, for immediately after, the tragedian, clad in his ordinary clothes, stepped before the curtain, and in a quiet, patient, and penitent manner intimated his wish to explain himself. A wild howl as from a pack of hungry wolves greeted him, and was followed by a shower of cabbages, oranges, and small brass buttons the size of musket-bullets, some of which struck him; water squirted from syringes, and the contents of bottles containing "offensive drugs" were also flung at him. Surprised, indignant, and alarmed, Kean withdrew.

A general demand was then made for the manager, when Mr. Kilner appeared, and was heard to say Kean "wished to make an apology from his heart and soul;" on which a response was roared by some avenger of outraged virtue, "Damn his soul." Kean came forward, but the yells which uprose caused him to retire unheard. Kilner then re-entered with a placard announcing, "Mr. Kean declines playing;" and having waited until this was seen by all, turned its reverse side, on which was written, "Shall the play go on without him?" To this no

RIOT IN THE THEATRE.

answer was made; the storm, however, continued, even after the curtain drew up and the tragedy of *Richard III.* began. But seeing a substitute for Kean had been provided, a wild cry went up from the rioters, who feared their victim had escaped. Again and again he was called for, when one of the actors stated he had left the theatre.

The play was now stopped, for a fresh excitement occurred. The hundreds blocking the streets outside being unable to gain admission, determined to force an entrance at all risks. The doors which had been closed and barred were violently forced open, and the pit being incapable of holding another individual, the intruders pushed their way up the stairs leading to the boxes. Between the occupants of these and the new-comers skirmishes followed, doors were smashed, windows broken, and escape by the ordinary channel becoming impossible, those who considered their only safety lay in flight jumped from a window in the second story, a distance of ten feet, on to a wooden shed below, and from that into the street. Those who remained to brave the battle were gradually forced into the pit, and those in the pit on to the stage. From there they rushed behind the scenes, with a cry for Kean! Kean! hungering like wild beasts for their prey. The tragedian had fortunately withdrawn from the house, and taken refuge in the residence of the prompter, George Clarke, which adjoined and communicated with the theatre, and his pursuers, rendered furious by his escape, ran into the dressing-rooms and the wardrobe, where, donning helmets and arming themselves with halberds, pikes, and swords, they hastened back to the stage. The spirit of warfare now having possession of them, they seized the brackets and branches supporting the chandeliers, wrenched them from their positions, and deliberately broke the lustres with their pikes. Bricks and stones were flung from without through the windows with disastrous effects; benches were torn up, the curtains of boxes rent to shreds, and finally the gas was extinguished.

Long before the rioters had proceeded so far the police had sought to interfere with them, but they were powerless against such numbers. The manager then sent for Mayor Quincy, with a request that he would read the Riot Act, but that worthy individual preferred safety at home to danger abroad; Mr. Justice Whitman was then urgently requested to come to the rescue, and he, forcing his way to the stage, twice read the Riot Act, when the theatre was saved from utter destruction. Throughout the night the streets were thronged by excited mobs; the ringleaders of which, suspecting

Kean was in George Clarke's house, made several attempts to enter with the intention of dragging him out and inflicting vengeance on him, but Mr. Southworth, a gallant man, stood upon the steps of the dwelling, and when the infuriated rioters presented themselves, assured them Kean was not there. Then appealing to their manhood and gallantry, he told them Mrs. Clarke, who hourly expected to become a mother, was in an extremely critical condition, and begged them to depart. About one o'clock that morning Kean, being disguised, made his escape through Theatre Alley, and was conveyed to the Exchange Coffee-House. Here he was placed under the protection of two stout fellows named Perkins and Collamore. His fear was great, for it was rumoured the brutal mob, who intended to tar and feather him, were on his track, and it was with a grateful heart he, with his two companions, set out in the small hours of the morning for Providence. From there he travelled to Worcester, and then went to New York, where he arrived worn by fatigue, and prostrate with grief.

The good people of Boston prided themselves on having driven him from their midst, and the *Boston Courier* flung a last stone after him. "Two weeks ago," said this chaste organ, "we did not believe that our managers would have been guilty of so much contempt for public opinion, and so much disregard for public decency as to permit Kean to play on their stage, but we find ourselves deceived. Four days ago too we did not believe that so worthless a fellow, such a double-faced beggar for 'an asylum in which to end his professional and mortal career,' would have confidence enough to raise so much feeling on his account."

Kean's condition was now most pitiful; at home and abroad, he who by his genius had given the highest intellectual pleasure in the power of no other man to bestow in equal measure, was treated in a cruel and barbarous manner. Home or country he had none: he had been repudiated for a fault until his punishment assumed the shape of persecution.

He sufficiently rallied his spirits to play on the 4th of January, 1826, at New York for the benefit of Mrs. Hilson. The house was crowded, and, as if to atone in part for the brutal conduct he had recently experienced, the audience was most enthusiastic. At the end of the performance he was called forward, and in a few words referred with warmth and pain to his reception at Boston.

The character he represented on this occasion was that of King Lear, and next day, upon his old friend Dr. Francis congratulating him on his success, Kean said the decrepitude and insanity of Lear rendered it a laborious part, and told him, that in order to study various effects of insanity he had visited some madhouses in London. " By the way," he added, " I understand you have an asylum for lunatics here, which I should like to visit."

The doctor being willing to gratify him, a few days later they, acompanied by a mutual friend, drove to the Bloomingdale asylum. On their way they passed some famous public gardens known as Vauxhall, which the tragedian expressed a desire to see. He therefore gravely descended from his carriage, and asked the gate-keeper if he might walk over the grounds, but before a reply could be made Kean had turned a double somersault, to the wonder and consternation of the porter, and in a second stood at a considerable distance. There he quietly waited his friends, admired the grounds, and then continued his drive. Arriving at the asylum, he was introduced to the officials, and with them visited the patients under their care. Before quitting the building, he was told that if he ascended to the roof he would obtain a magnificent view of the surrounding counties. Delighted with the idea, he and his companions went on the roof, and Kean expressed his admiration of the wide prospect of hill and dale, woodland and winding river spreading before him. Suddenly he exclaimed, "I'll walk to the ridge of the roof and make a leap, it is the best end I can make of my life," and away he rushed towards the western gable; but his friends hurrying after him, seized him and brought him back, nor did they lose sight of him until they left him, apparently in a calmer mood, at his hotel. It is notable that had he succeeded in his resolution to leap from the roof, he would have died in the same fashion as his father had long ago.

"I have ever been at a loss," said Dr. Francis, who narrates this incident, "to account for this sudden freak in his feelings; he was buoyant at the outset of the journey, he astonished the Vauxhall gate-keeper by his harlequin trick, and took an interest in the various forms of insanity which came before him. He might have become too sublimated in his feelings, or had his senses unsettled (for he was an electrical apparatus) in contemplating the mysterious influences acting on the minds of the deranged, for there is an attractive principle as well as an adhesive principle in madness; or a crowd of thoughts might have oppressed him, arising from the disaster which had occurred to him a few days before with the Boston audience, and the irreparable loss he had sustained in the plunder of his trunks and valuable papers while journeying hither and thither on his return to New York."

From this city he resolved to visit Philadelphia, but Wood, the theatrical manager, wrote to him, that whilst the present excitement continued, if he came to Philadelphia he would not be answerable for the consequences; Kean therefore, though advertised to appear, absented himself. On the evening of the 9th of January, when he was to have begun his engagement, Wood, on being called for, stated it was not only his desire but his interest that Kean would act in his theatre, but he was powerless to drag him before an audience. If he declined to perform a manager had no power to compel him. Now an English actor named Francis Courtney Wemyss, who was indebted to Kean for many acts of kindness, happening to know what had passed between Wood and the tragedian, stated to several influential men of the city that Kean would come if assured of his personal safety, but that Wood had written him word his life would be endangered by his visit. Inquiries followed, when the stage-manager was despatched to interview Kean, who came to Philadelphia, and made his appearance at the theatre as Richard III. on the 18th of January, 1826.

The scene which followed his entrance on the stage

was disgraceful. Rotten eggs, oranges, buttons, and other missiles were flung at him, in the midst of which he stood calm and sorrowful, so distressed in outward seeming that his worst enemy might have pitied him. Unable to obtain a hearing, he retired amidst a triumphant yell of hate. The tragedy then began, and was continued in pantomime, the noise drowning all sound of the players' voices, until at length, wearied by exertion, the tumult became gradually less. Then Kean, seeing his opportunity, stepped from the centre of the stage to the front, and said, "Friends of the drama, this is your quarrel, not mine." This statement, together with his admirable playing, had the effect of quieting them, so that the last acts of *Richard III.* were heard in silence. When the curtain fell an immense crowd gathered round the stage door to see the tragedian leave the theatre; whether their purpose was to cheer or groan it was impossible to say, but as he was about to enter his carriage one of his friends cried out for "Three cheers for Kean!" to which the mob, previously hesitating in its course, immediately responded.

From that evening forward, during the fortnight he played in Philadelphia, he was listened to with attention and applauded with heartiness; so that on the last night of his engagement he made the following speech when the curtain fell—" Ladies and gentlemen, my life has been a chequered one, at one time reaching the pinnacle of ambition, at another sunk to the lowest ebb of misfortune. I appeared before you at the beginning of my present engagement, sick and dejected by the gloom which the malignity of enemies had thrown around me, anxious and willing to resign the contest; but the kindness of a Philadelphian audience has dispelled these visions of despair, and I hope I shall have the honour early next season of appearing before this kind auditory."

At Baltimore he was not so fortunate; indeed, the scene of his first night's appearance in that town was but a repetition of what he had experienced at Boston, for he was neither permitted to play nor to speak; and as it was believed personal violence would be offered him, he was conveyed from the theatre through an adjoining house to his hotel. He then returned to New York, and was next engaged by Simpson and Cowell, managers of the Charleston Theatre, to play in that town. Joe Cowell had some time previously left England, and becoming popular in America, had embarked in management. Admiring Kean as a great tragedian, and sympathizing with him as a persecuted man, he sought by every means in his power to secure him a peaceful if not an enthusiastic reception at Charleston. He had, however, to contend with a hostile press, which declared this unfortunate man should be hounded out of the country.

Kean having sailed in the middle of February for Charleston in the ship *Othello*, Joe Cowell hastened to greet him on his arrival. "I boarded the vessel before she crossed the bar," says the manager, "and found this wreck of better days feeble in body, and that brilliant poetic face a Raphael might have envied for a study, 'sicklied o'er with the pale cast of thought.' His first inquiry was if the public were hostile to his appearance; and like a child he appealed to me, 'Cowell, for God's sake, by the ties of old fellowship and countrymen, I entreat you not to let me play if you think the audience will not receive me. I have not strength of mind or body—look how I am changed since you saw me last—to endure a continuance of the persecutions I have already suffered, and I believe a repetition of them would kill me on the spot.'"

Cowell encouraged him to hope all would be well, and he seemed pacified, until on landing from their boat some idlers who had collected there hissed and groaned. "The well-known hateful sound," Cowell says, "seemed to enter his very soul, and looking up in my face, with 'God help me,' quivering on his parted lips, he clung to my arm as if for succour, not support. I assured him the disapprobation was meant for an officer of the customs, in whose boat we had landed, who was objectionable to the people, and doubting, yet hoping, it was true, led him to my house."

Throughout the night he never closed his eyes; his anxiety concerning his reception was great, and his rest was such

> "As wretches have o'er night
> Who wait for execution in the morn."

Next day he anxiously questioned all who approached him concerning the possible greeting that awaited him that evening, and his soul hung between hope and fear. Not a seat was booked, but on the doors of the theatre being opened, the house was soon crowded. On his entrance he was received with perfect silence, and throughout the night neither hissing nor clapping was heard. Kean's delight at this escape from the fate he dreaded was great, and next day every available place in the theatre was booked for his second appearance. But on this occasion some ill-advised persons vented their admiration in applause, which was instantly overwhelmed by hisses; then a pent-up storm burst over the house, yells and groans filled the air, oranges and apples were flung at the tragedian, and the curtain was lowered in the midst of a scene. Cowell then appeared, quietly picked up the missiles thrown on the stage, and with looks of indignation and regret bowed and withdrew. The curtain was again raised, and the scene continued; Kean was suffered to proceed, and before the tragedy of *Othello* had concluded, the house was unanimous in its stormy applause. He had conquered prejudice.

Next day some of the first men in the city left their cards at his hotel; dinner-parties were arranged for him, carriages were placed at his service, fruits and flowers were sent him in abundance, and his share of the receipts of the houses to which he played amounted to two hundred and twenty-two dollars, or upwards of fifty pounds a night. So blessed a change was this to a man who had been hounded from town to town, that he resolved to stay here some time. Accordingly a friend gave him the use of a country house on Sullivan's Island—a sandbank in the centre of the harbour, uninhabited at this time of year, except by a few soldiers stationed at the fort. Here, with a couple of Newfoundland dogs, a horse, and a pet deer, he remained, striving to recover from the effects of his persecution, until May, when he returned again to New York.

Later on he visited Montreal and Quebec, and was favourably received in both towns. Before his departure from the former he was entertained at a public dinner at the Masonic Hall Hotel, and in the course of a speech made in reply to the drinking of his health, spoke of his departure from England in a manner that serves to throw fresh light upon his many-sided character. "I was scarcely from the land," he said, "when reason told me I had lost a portion of my respectability as a man, and my chief resources depended on my exertions as an actor. I assumed, therefore, a callous indifference, played for a time the character of a misanthrope, knit my brows, and pretended contempt for the world, but it was merely acting. Deeply I felt the loss of that society I had for years associated with, and every little act of kindness penetrated the brazen armour I had borrowed for the occasion. The searching eye could soon discern smiles without mirth, and pastime without pleasure."

At Quebec his advent excited unusual interest. He had been announced to perform on Monday, the 8th of September, and expected to arrive on the previous Thursday; but neither did he appear on that day, nor on Friday, Saturday, or Sunday, and this disappointment increased the sensation already excited. On Monday, however, news was brought that he was positively in the tug-boat *Hercules*, which was towing a vessel into the harbour, when a number of citizens went down to meet and give him a hearty welcome; and the manager, learning that he was willing and able to play that night, sent the public bellman round to announce the fact. The theatre was crowded, the governor, Lady Dalhousie and suite occupied boxes, and Kean was enthusiastically applauded.

During his engagement here an incident occurred which greatly delighted him. Becoming aware of the excitement his performances created, a number of Indians attended the theatre; when Kean, gratified by their visit, and pleased by their picturesque appearance, desired to become better acquainted with them. Introductions therefore followed. He was no less an object of wonder and admiration to them than they were to him. Acquaintanceship soon ripened to intimacy; he entertained them hospitably, recited for them, sang and played to them, rode with and tumbled for them, and finally expressed his desire to become one of the tribe, and leave the ways of the white man for ever. Impressed by the charm of his manner and his wonderful talents, they made him a chief, and with much ceremony invested him with a costume such as they wore, and gave him the name of Alanienouidet. He then disappeared with them. Subsequently speaking of this period to his friend Grattan, he declared he had gone mad for several days, and having joined the Indians in their camp, he was pursued by some friends who carried him back, and for a considerable time treated him as a lunatic, before he was allowed to leave for New York.

Soon after it happened that Dr. Francis, late one evening, received a message requesting he would call upon the renowned Indian chief, Alanienouidet, then staying at an hotel close at hand. Hastening to obey the summons, the doctor soon arrived at the chief's temporary residence, and being silently conducted upstairs, was left at the folding-doors of a large apartment, when the servant mysteriously disappeared. He then entered the lofty room, which was but dimly lighted, and looking round, saw at the far end a forest of palms, ferns, and evergreens illuminated by lamps, which, placed upon the floor, threw their rays upon a great throne, on which was the seated figure of a warrior chief. His appearance was strikingly picturesque. His small, well-shaped head was decked with eagle plumes, from behind which masses of black locks flowed on his shoulders; thick gold rings hung from his nose and ears, his face was streaked with red and yellow paint, a collar of bear-skins clasped his neck, buffalo hides clad his form; his leggings were garnished with porcupine quills, his mocassins decorated with beads, his bare arms adorned with shining bracelets; a tomahawk was suspended from a broad belt round his waist, whilst in his hands he held a bow and arrow.

Seeing his visitor enter, he gravely descended from his throne and approached him. "His eye," says the doctor, "was meteoric and fearful, like the furnace of the Cyclops. He vociferously exclaimed Alanienouidet, the vowels strong enough. I was relieved; he betrayed something of his rancous voice in imprecation. It was Kean." He was as rejoiced as a school-boy at the impression he made, and the effect of his costume; declared he valued the honour the Indians had conferred on him above the highest triumph he had achieved at Drury Lane; and that he was yet undecided whether he would wholly cast his lot with them, or return to London.

On Monday the 18th of November, 1826, he played Richard III. at the Park Theatre before a crowded audience, whose enthusiasm showed that all ill-feeling towards him had ended. During the week he played Othello and Shylock, but scarce had he finished the representation of the latter character, when he was taken ill in the green-room with violent spasmodic attacks. That he had suffered deeply, both mentally and physically, was but too apparent; his powers had declined, and by some of his acquaintances it was considered he had not long to live. Commenting on these facts, the *Albion* stated, that nothing but a salutary and persevering reform in his social habits could prolong his existence. "Possibly," it adds, "the abstinence of a sea voyage, the counsel of his friends, and the suggestions of his own good sense may work a beneficial change in some of his injurious indulgences."

Early in December it was announced by the press that, in consequence of information recently received from England, Kean was about to return immediately to that country, and had taken his passage on board the ship *Silas Richards*, which sailed on the 8th of the month. He therefore made his last appearance in America on Tuesday, December 5th, 1826, in the part of Richard III.

CHAPTER VI.

Changes at Drury Lane—The new manager—Kean's reception by the public—Indications of ill-health—Grattan's tragedy of *Ben Nazir*—A morning visit to the tragedian—Studying his part—A painful performance—A shadowed life—Young Charles Kean—His engagement at Drury Lane—First appearance—Severity of the critics—Acting in Dublin—Three cheers for a speech—Edmund Kean in Paris—Reconciled to his son—Charles Kean plays Romeo—The elder Kean at Covent Garden—The cry of a despairing soul—At Bute—A pitiful letter—Quarrels with the management of Covent Garden.

WHILST Edmund Kean was in America some changes had taken place in Drury Lane. Owing to the expenditure consequent on the rebuilding, improving, and decorating of the theatre, and the poor receipts of some unprofitable seasons, Elliston had become deeply involved in debt. Aware of this, the shareholders called a meeting in May, 1826, when a demand was made that the lessee should pay within three days the arrears of rent, amounting to five thousand five hundred pounds.

During his term of management Elliston had paid sixty-six thousand pounds for rent; and though, by the conditions of his agreement, he was not compelled to spend more than seven thousand pounds in improving the house, he had already expended almost four times that sum. The portico in Brydges Street, erected from designs by Sir John Soane, cost over a thousand pounds, and the reconstructing of the interior of the theatre, improvements of the stage, and lining the saloon with looking-glasses, required an outlay of twenty-two thousand pounds. Elliston therefore considered this prompt demand for the balance of rent from those whose property he had greatly enhanced, exceedingly harsh; but the shareholders were unflinching, and the meeting was adjourned for three days. At the end of that time Elliston submitted proposals from a committee of his creditors, who were ready to give security for the amount he owed; the shareholders, however, would not listen to this suggestion, and insisted that Elliston should either pay the money down or resign his lesseeship; therefore the Napoleon of Drury Lane was obliged to enter the Bankruptcy Court, and the national theatre knew him no more.

Offers were then invited for the lesseeship, which was finally granted to Stephen Price, an American, known in the theatrical profession as the "Star provider to the United States," he having acted as an agent for some American theatres in which he had an interest. Now, whilst Kean was in New York, he received a letter purporting to come from Stephen Price, asking him to return immediately and take possession of the management of Drury Lane Theatre, which was only held in trust for "its true inheritor." He had therefore hastened to England, and arriving in January, 1827, learned the communication was merely a hoax.

His disappointment was great, but was somewhat alleviated by an offer to play at Drury Lane for twelve nights at fifty pounds a night. It was therefore announced that Mr. Kean, having arrived from America to fulfil an engagement for a limited number of nights, would make his first appearance on the 8th of January in the character of Shylock. On this evening the theatre was crowded to excess; long before the curtain rose cries for "Kean, Kean," were heard from every part of the house, and the moment the play began a shout was sent up, says the *Morning Chronicle*, "sufficient to fright the realm of chaos and old night, in which every voice joined." Again and again was Kean called for during the first scene, until at last he came forward, when a deafening roar broke over the house; the pit rose, handkerchiefs and hats were waved from circle and gallery, and cheers literally shook the building. Overcome by emotion caused by the contrast of this reception to that which the same people had given him but a little while before, Kean stood gazing at them calmly, a smile, it might be of disdain or gratification, on his lips. Then, turning to the stage, he began his performance.

It was considered he had never acted so ably; the parts in which he was wont to use great physical exertions were now softened and subdued, a change which was regarded as an improvement. He was warmly applauded throughout, and at the fall of the curtain was loudly called for; but he was evidently not willing to comply with the wishes of his audience. One of the actors came forward, as if desirous of apologizing for Kean's non-appearance, but vainly solicited a hearing, on which he withdrew. The applause and cries for Kean continuing, the tragedian at last appeared. He had changed Shylock's garberdine for his own clothes, and removed the paint from his face, when it was noted for the first time how pale, worn, and haggard he appeared. On a general demand being made for a speech, he merely bowed again and again, and quietly made his exit. Three nights later he acted Othello when he was as enthusiastically received as on, the previous occasion; but it was noticed he played with languor, and that many of his speeches were delivered mechanically, rather than with his former enthusiasm. Later still, when he personated Richard III., it was painfully evident he was physically a wreck of his former self; the old spirit which had kindled his audience to fervour was often absent, whilst the traces of suffering were but too visible.

And being now dependent on his present earnings, which were squandered by his extravagant habits as soon as received, he was obliged to work when rest was necessary to his restoration to health. He therefore accepted an engagement to play in Dublin, but the effects of dissipation were sadly perceptible, and his audiences regarded him with compassion and regret. At this time he suffered, amongst other ailments, from a sore leg, for which he was attended by Surgeon Carpue, who prescribed the strictest *régime*, and commanded abstinence from all strong liquors, directions his patient strove hard to follow. By nursing himself for two consecutive days, he was able to play three times a week; but even then the exertion of acting caused him great pain and fatigue.

To commemorate his return to Dublin, the patentee, committee, and performers of the Theatre Royal commissioned an artist named Feyer to paint a full-length portrait of Kean, representing him, at his own request, as an Indian chief. Of the honour the tribe had conferred on him he was yet proud, and when he took his benefit on the 2nd of April, it was announced he would not only play King Lear, but deliver a farewell address in the character and costume of Alanienouidet, chief of the Huron Indians; which name and title, says the playbills, "were conferred upon him by a full assembly of the tribe at Quebec in 1826."

In May he was back again at Drury Lane, filling a regular engagement. The while his health varied, little progress being made towards recovery, and during the season an event occurred which showed how much his recent troubles had affected his mental and physical condition.

When three years previously Kean had met his old friend Grattan at Boulogne, he asked him if he had ever thought of writing for the stage. In reply Grattan stated he had once attempted a tragedy, the hero of which he hoped might be played by him, but he had long ago laid it aside; he would, however, if Kean promised to read the manuscript, re-write it, and send it him. On this the tragedian promised he would use every exertion to have it brought forward with all possible advantage. The trial which soon after followed, together with Kean's reception by the public, and his subsequent visit to America, caused the tragedy to be laid aside. But Kean having returned to London, and being enthusiastically welcomed, Grattan forwarded his play, *Ben Nazir the Saracen*, and a few days later called on Kean, who was then living at the Hummums Hotel, Covent Garden.

Grattan found him sitting up in bed, a buffalo skin wrapped round him, a huge fur cap decked with many gorgeous feathers on his head, a scalping knife in his belt, and a tomahawk in his hand. A tumbler of white wine negus was within his reach, two shabby-looking boon companions bore him company, whilst an artist painted his portrait as Alanienouidet. Grattan was announced by a negro boy in livery, and on his entrance Kean gave a ferocious roll of his eyes, flourished his tomahawk, threw off his cap, and shook his visitor warmly by the hand. The boon companions now retired, the painter laid down his brushes, and Kean told his friend he had read *Ben Nazir*, and from six manuscripts submitted to him by the manager, amongst which was Sheridan Knowles's play of *Alfred*, he had selected it as the piece in which he would make his "regenerated appearance" before a London public. He then produced from under his pillow the part of *Ben Nazir*, which he was committing to memory; for it was stipulated in his new engagement at Drury Lane that he should be ready to play in this tragedy early in May, and he trusted this representation would confirm him in the favour lately accorded him by the public. His flow of conversation was interrupted by the entrance of the black boy, who ushered in two ladies heavily veiled; these Kean assured his friend, in a stage whisper, were two lovely creatures, the daughters of a clergyman of high respectability, who, having fallen desperately in love with him, came to London to offer him their affections. Hearing which Grattan took his leave.

Later he paid the tragedian several visits, and having many opportunities of observing him, came to the conclusion that "his whole situation, appearance, and conduct at this critical period of his career were very remarkable and characteristic. He presented a mixture of subdued fierceness, unsatisfied triumph, and suppressed debauchery. He had in a great measure recovered his place before the public, but he had lost all the respectability of private life. His health had been greatly shattered during his American campaign, chiefly, I believe, from his mental sufferings."

Rehearsals of *Ben Nazir* were now begun, and the

players who had been cast for the piece were perfect in their parts with the exception of Kean, who read his speeches with great vigour, and produced a powerful impression on his hearers. From the later rehearsals he absented himself, stating he was unwilling to lose time from the close study he wished to give the minutest details of his representation. There could be no doubt he laboured hard to impress the words upon his memory, for he daily drove to Kensington Gardens, where he studied quietly for a couple of hours, a practice he varied by taking a boat, and whilst being rowed towards Greenwich recited his speeches with dramatic effect. His enthusiasm regarding Ben Nazir was great; he was certain he should play it a hundred nights during the season; he laid out fifty guineas over and above the sum allowed him by the manager for his costumes; he declared he would have his portrait painted and engraved as Ben Nazir, a name by which he would call the new boat he was about to present as a prize for the annual wherry race he had instituted.

The night for the performance of the tragedy was at length fixed. Kean stated he was quite prepared, but refused to appear at the last rehearsals, saying it would not only confuse and annoy him, but perhaps destroy the effect he wished to reserve for the public. The town thronged to see the new play, and the author, full of high hopes, sat in a private box at the back of the dress-circle. The curtain rose, the tragedy began, and the house waited for Kean with breathless anxiety. Meanwhile, as the first scene proceeded the call-boy summoned the tragedian, who failed to make his appearance; again and again the call was given, but with like effect, until seriously alarmed, the manager rushed to Kean's dressing-room, where he found him "weeping and in total despair;" he could not remember his part. It was now too late to postpone the play, and whatever the consequences, he must go on the stage; therefore, when the drop curtain rose on the second scene, he was discovered clad in a magnificent dress, his arms folded on his breast, his attitude one of thoughtful solemnity.

Thunders of applause greeted him from all parts of the house. "Then he spoke," says Grattan, "but what a speech. The one I wrote consisted of eight or nine lines; his was of two or three sentences, but not six consecutive words of the text. His look, his manner, his tone were to me quite appalling; to any other observer they must have been incomprehensible. He stood fixed, drawled out his incoherent words, and gave the notion of a man who had been half-hanged, and then dragged through a horsepond. My heart, I confess it, sank deep in my breast; I was utterly shocked. And as the business of the play went on, and as he stood by with moveless muscle and glazed eye, throughout the scene which should have been one of violent exertion, a cold shower of perspiration poured from my forehead, and I endured a revulsion of feeling which I cannot describe, and which I would not for worlds one eye had witnessed. I had all along felt that this scene would be the touchstone of the play. Kean went through it like a man in the last stage of exhaustion and decay. The act closed, a dead silence followed the fall of the curtain, and I felt, though I could not hear, the voiceless verdict of damnation."

As the tragedy continued it was evident to all something had gone wrong; for Kean was not only defective in the knowledge of the lines he ought to have delivered, but in the utterance of those for which his memory served him. No spark was visible of that genius which had lighted him to fame; no trace was present of that power which had moved thousands. "A contemplation of the wreck of great energies is always mournful," said a morning paper, speaking of this performance, "but in the present instance it reached a point which was absolutely afflicting."

At the fall of the curtain there were signs of impatience and disappointment; and on the manager coming forward, he had some difficulty in obtaining silence. When allowed to speak, he said he had been commissioned by Mr. Kean to apologize for his ignorance of his part; the mental anxiety and bodily illness from which he had suffered had so far impaired his powers of memory as to prevent him doing justice to the author. Grattan, now leaving his box, took his way with a heavy heart behind the scenes, and crossing the stage met Kean supported by two men, who were leading him to his dressing-room. He hung his head, and waving his hand said, "I have ruined a fine play and myself; I cannot look you in the face." The poor author strove to say something consolatory, for his sense of disappointment was lost in compassion for the wreck he beheld. The tragedy met its fate, and was never revived.

Mrs. Kean, now separated from her husband, lived in lodgings in Rider Street, St. James's, on an allowance of two hundred a year, which he, though still profuse in his expenditure, and notable for his generosity, grudgingly allowed her. The misfortune which had fallen on him shadowed her life, and, broken-spirited and ill, she lived in close retirement. Her son was still at Eton, which he had entered in June, 1824, having previously been sent to preparatory schools at Thames Ditton and at Greenford. His parents had intended him for one of two professions—his mother's inclination being to make him a clergyman, whilst his father desired he should enter the navy. As he was soon, at the end of his three years' residence there, to leave Eton, Edmund Kean requested Mr. Calcraft, a member of Parliament, and formerly one of the Drury Lane Committee, to procure a cadetship for the lad in the East India Company's service. Calcraft promised to exert his influence towards obliging his old friend, and Kean resolved his son should obey his wishes, irrespective of his own inclinations.

But some months before Charles was to leave Eton, his mother, hearing of her husband's intentions, sent for the lad, and implored him, as he loved her, not to part from her now she was afflicted by illness and oppressed by grief. This he readily promised, and seeking his father, told him he could not leave his mother sick and helpless, and he must decline acceptance of the cadetship. The tragedian, who listened to him, coldly asked if he were aware that in declining the appointment he gave him up; to which Charles replied, it was impossible to believe his father could be angry with him for acting as he did.

"What will you do when you are thrown entirely on

your own resources?" Kean asked, to which his son answered, he should be compelled to seek his fortune on the stage, where he could at least obtain a livelihood for himself and his mother without being under an obligation to any one. At this reply Kean became furious, declaring he would be the first and last actor of his name, and would never see his son any more. Under these circumstances they parted, and all intimacy between them ceased. Mrs. Kean then wrote to inform Mr. Calcraft of her son's resolution, and received from him the following reply—

"*Hanover Square, Feb. 27th,* 1827.

"DEAR MADAM,

"I confess it was a great disappointment to me that you and your son refused (if it could be obtained) the cadetship to the East Indies, for after what you have said, I did not expect it. Yet, having been much pleased with your son's manner and appearance, and being thoroughly sensible of his unprotected situation, I shall not withhold from him any services which may be in my power. Always wishing you to keep in mind that I am entirely without official interest.

"I am, dear Madam,

"Your obedient servant,

"J. CALCRAFT."

The following July Charles left Eton for good, and going to his mother's lodgings, found her not only in illness but in poverty, the annuity her husband had previously allowed her being stopped. Without resources or expectations, sorrowful and ill, her condition was pitiable; but an occurrence soon happened that filled her with hope. A little while before Edmund Kean had quarrelled with Stephen Price, and had entered into negotiations with Charles Kemble, now manager of Covent Garden Theatre. Hearing of Charles Kean's intention of becoming an actor, and believing the son of the great tragedian would prove attractive to the town, Price made the lad, now in his sixteenth year, an offer of an engagement for three years at a salary of ten pounds a week, with a promise of increasing that sum to eleven and twelve pounds a week during the second and third year in case he proved successful. This was gladly and gratefully accepted, and Charles began to prepare himself for his new duties.

Drury Lane Theatre opened for the winter season on Monday the 1st of October, 1827, on which occasion Mr. Kean, junior, as he was termed in the play-bills, made his first appearance on any stage as Young Norval in the tragedy of *Douglas*. A brilliant and fashionable house assembled to witness his *début*. On his entrance he was greeted with a loud burst of applause, which seemed to unnerve him, for he stood motionless, "excepting," says the *Morning Chronicle*, "that the timid heavings of his chest could be distinctly observed from all parts of the house." But soon recovering himself, he began his part, and retained his self-possession to the end.

In appearance he was merely a stripling of five feet seven inches, slightly built, and strongly resembling his father in the upper part of his face. His voice was yet lacking in fullness and sweetness, his undertones being almost inaudible, and he expressed but little feeling; his actions, however, were in general free, unconstrained, and graceful. There was much indeed in his person and manner to recall the great actor whose name he bore; but the withering glance, the musical tones, and the impassioned gesture of the elder Kean were wanting, and all comparison between them was calculated to prove the inferiority of this youth. Though the tragedy wanted novelty and interest, and the hero strength and experience, his delivery of many passages was greeted with applause, and at the fall of the curtain the manager, on coming forward, was not allowed to speak until he retired and led Charles Kean forward to receive the hearty congratulations of his friendly audience.

Next day the criticisms of the press, with the exception of the *Morning Chronicle*, were marked by severity; the *Times* being especially bitter in its remarks, as if determined to continue on his son the malignity with which it had ever treated the elder Kean; and reading over its remarks, the young actor and his mother cried bitterly. "We have heard," says this organ, "and we give credit to the statement, that the elder Kean had provided for his son by procuring him an appointment in the East India Company's Service. If it be not too late, we should advise the young gentleman to push his fortune in the East, and if he needs must be theatrical, he may amuse himself on the Chowringhee stage, and on many other stages in India, where amateur performances are greatly admired. . . . With respect to his voice and his style of declamation, we can say nothing favourable. The former is weak, unmusical, and puerile; the latter better adapted to the conventicle than to the stage. It is tedious, drawling, and monotonous, such as well-whipped boys occasionally at Christmas exhibit before their delighted parents. Had it been any other than the son of one who has so often and so entirely gratified the public by his fine genius, the young gentleman would most assuredly have been driven from the boards with at least as much precipitancy as that with which the American manager has forced him on them."

The indulgence usually granted to novices was denied him by the press; no hope was held forward that experience and study would remedy his faults; the resemblance he bore his father was held up to remind him of his inefficiency; and but for the bitter necessity which existed for means to support himself and his mother, he would have retired from the stage, and have fallen a victim to the severity of critics. Stephen Price encouraged him to persevere, and pitying this lad who was friendless, hopeless, and untutored, gave him every assistance in his power. The tragedy of *Douglas* was repeated on the following Thursday, and later on he appeared as Achmet in *Barbarossa*, and Frederick in *Lover's Vows;* but the audiences to which he played becoming thinner and thinner, the friendly manager advised him to go into the provinces until he gained experience.

He therefore crossed over to Ireland, and made his appearance at the Dublin Theatre as Norval; here he was warmly received, and at the fall of the curtain a general demand was made for a speech. Frightened at the prospect of addressing the house, and aware it was impossible to refuse the request without risk of offence, he began, "Ladies and Gentlemen, I am deeply sensible of your being quite unprepared—no, I mean of my being quite unprepared—ahem, quite incapable of thanks totally unmerited—never to be effaced when time shall be no more—" Having arrived at this climax of incoherence, one of the gods shouted out, "That'll do, Charlie, me boy; go home to your mother." As he on this dismissal bowed and took his departure, a call was made for "Three cheers for Charlie Kean's speech," to which the house thoroughly responded.

Meanwhile, Edmund Kean had retired to Wood Cottage, Bute, without coming to conclusive terms with Charles Kemble, to whom he presently wrote, inviting him on a visit. This the latter declined, but sent him proposals for his appearance at Covent Garden Theatre. In answer Kean said—

"My dear Sir,

"Your letter confirms my first impression of your character, namely, that you are a good man and a good actor. Your kindness in the first instance of our meeting cannot be erased; and the second is placed on the monument of memory. I regret in your letter telling me you cannot visit Bute. Shakespeare, you, and I, I think, would form most excellent companionship (*Pares cum paribus facillime congregantur*). But I shall obey your injunctions, and fortify my constitutional batteries against the new campaign.

"My dear Sir,
"With sincere respect,
"EDMUND KEAN.

"P.S.—I accept the proposals made by the managers of the Theatre Royal, Covent Garden. I had nearly forgot all this."

Whilst his son was in Dublin, Edmund Kean appeared on the 15th October, 1827, at Covent Garden as Shylock. He was received with enthusiasm, and it seemed as if his audience was resolved to crown his unrivalled talents with new triumph on his displaying them at this house. Throughout the performance he was interrupted by the warmest applause, and at the conclusion, when Charles Kemble came forward to announce the play for the next evening, he was greeted with cries for Kean, on which he retired, but presently returned to state that, not feeling well, and being greatly exhausted by his exertions, Kean had quitted the house immediately after his performance; he added, that though it was impossible for Mr. Kean to answer the call made upon him, there could be no doubt he would be highly flattered on learning the desire of his audience.

Throughout the winter his appearance at Covent Garden was frequently interrupted by illness; but in the spring of the year 1828 he was sufficiently recovered to give some performances at Paris. As early as 1822 an English company had appeared at the Porte St. Martin Theatre, but on their attempt to perform had been hooted from the stage, on which a tumult arose that almost ended in bloodshed; for the Parisians had borne in mind, that a company of French dancers engaged by David Garrick to appear in a performance called a *Chinese Festival*, about the middle of the previous century, had met with most uncivil treatment from the English people.

Six years later another attempt to challenge Parisian criticism was made by an English company, which included, amongst others, Macready, Miss Smithson, Abbott, and Webster. Their efforts were well received, but the French public being unused to Shakespearean performances, were not wholly appreciative of the dramatist's genius, and when Macready acted Macbeth, the witches were received with peals of laughter; moreover, in the cauldron scene, where mention is made of the ingredients thrown into it, a horrified Frenchman shouted out, *O Mon Dieu, quel mélange.*

On Edmund Kean being announced to play, curiosity to see him was great. His first appearance was made in the character of Richard III., but the Parisians, long used to the cold declamatory style, did not fully appreciate his stirring acting and passionate outbursts, and a mutual sense of disappointment ensued. For his second appearance he was advertised to play Othello. A crowded audience awaited him, but he was not to be found; the distracted manager sent messengers in search of him, one of whom discovered him contentedly drinking cognac in the Café Anglais. On being told a great house expected him, Kean, who had already drank too much brandy, replied, he did not care a fig. "But," replied the messenger, "the Duchess de Berri has arrived." "I am not a servant of the Duchess," he replied. "More brandy."

After much persuasion he was induced to quit the *café* and go to the theatre, but when he appeared upon the stage his condition became plain to the audience. At the next night of his appearance a poor house assembled to see him, on which he threw up his engagement and went to Bute, which he made his head-quarters during the summer, fulfilling short engagements now and then in London and the provinces. Whilst at Bute in the autumn, his son, who had meanwhile been working hard in the country, was announced to play at Glasgow, and being so near his father, Charles was desirous of visiting him, and establishing peace between them. A mutual friend undertook to aid the reconciliation, when Kean not only received his son, but offered to play for his benefit at the Glasgow Theatre. Accordingly, on the 1st of October, 1828, the anniversary of Charles's first appearance, both father and son acted in Howard Payne's tragedy of *Brutus*, before a densely-crowded house, the receipts of which amounted to almost three hundred pounds.

In the following month Edmund Kean was again performing at Covent Garden, representing his old characters, and drawing crowded houses whenever he appeared. But his habits were far from temperate, and his health was most uncertain. Occasionally he played mechanically, omitted many lines of his part, and made but slight impression, but again rallying his spirit, he would show he was still capable of exerting the charm which had fascinated audiences in happier days. George Vandenhoff, who was a boy at this period, speaks of seeing and remembering Kean.

"His style," he writes, "was impulsive, fitful, flashing, abounding in quick transitions; scarcely giving you time to think, but ravishing your wonder, and carrying you along with his impetuous rush and change of expression. But this seeming spontaneity was not chance work; much of it, most of it, was carefully premeditated and prepared. His delivery of Othello's farewell ran on the same tones and semi-tones, had the same rests and breaks, the same *forte* and *piano*, the same crescendo and diminuendo night after night as if he spoke it from a musical score. And what beautiful, what thrilling music it was—the music of a broken heart, the cry of a despairing soul."

In the December of this year Charles Kean, now in his seventeenth year, returned to Drury Lane, and father and son acted at the rival houses. Charles played Romeo to a new Juliet, and subsequently represented Frederick in *Lover's Vows* to the Amelia of Miss Ellen Tree, the lady who afterwards became his wife. His performances were still immature, and failed to attract audiences, whilst the press yet criticized him with unrelaxed severity. But he was now determined to become an actor, and again returned to the provinces, where he hoped practice would supply much that he required.

Early in January, 1829, Edmund Kean was obliged to retire for some time on account of his health, which became gradually worse, and going to his cottage in Bute, he busied himself in adorning his residence and improving its surroundings. But it was not only the condition of his health, but his association with an unprincipled and degraded woman, generally known as Ophelia, that caused grief and anxiety to his few remaining friends. Amongst those who most regretted the connection was his secretary Phillips, who had long striven to rescue Kean from his evil tendencies, and suffered much for sake of friendship. Seeing that the tragedian was not only fleeced of every pound he earned, but was likely to be robbed of the valuable mementoes presented him, he remonstrated with this heartless woman, who insulted him in so gross a manner that it was no longer possible for him to live under one roof with her. Knowing the influence she possessed over Kean, and believing any representations he might make regarding her would have no effect, he immediately left Bute cottage, and going to a neighbouring inn, wrote Kean a letter explaining his absence. In return he received the following pitiful reply—

"Dear Phillips,

"I am shocked, but not surprised. In error I was born, in error I have lived, in error I shall die. That a gentleman should be insulted under my roof creates a blush I shall carry with me to my grave; and that you are so in every sense of the word is unquestionable, from education, habits, and manners. It is too true that I have fostered a worm until it has become a viper; but my guilt is on my head. Farewell.

"Yours,
"Edmund Kean."

A short time afterwards he wrote to Tom Cunningham, then engaged at the Theatre Royal, Dublin—

"Dear Tom,

"I have read the Dublin Theatre is to be sold, and I suppose the greater part of the company left to starve or rob, according to their inclinations. Off with his head—so much for Berkley Bunn. Phillips has left me, and I feel quite at a loss for a friend and man of business. If you would like to spend the remainder of your days with me, correspond with the damned managers, and take care they don't swindle, I should be most happy to receive you. I would give you the precise terms I did Phillips—£50 per year, and as much bub and grub as you can stow in you, and the non-play days we will over pipe and glass laugh and defy the villainies and falsehoods of this world. I play next week in Manchester, from that to Edinburgh.

"Yours, dear Tom,

"Very sincerely,

"Edmund Kean.

"Ophelia sends her respects, and, like myself, would be very happy to see you."

Tom Cunningham, however, did not become his secretary, and the post was subsequently filled by Mr. Lee. In May, Edmund Kean had so far recovered as to be able to fulfil engagements in Dublin and Cork, where he again met and played in the same pieces with his son. But whilst in the former city he was so worn out "from general debility and disarrangement of the system," that the press declared his life was despaired of. From Ireland he went to Glasgow, where he played a few nights, and then retired to Bute. Here he became so seriously ill, that on one occasion a rumour of his death was spread. However, he rallied once more.

In October Charles returned to London, and filled an engagement at the Haymarket for six nights, when he played Romeo, Sir Edward Mortimer, and Reuben Glenroy with such success, that he was offered a permanent engagement by the manager, but this he wisely declined, preferring the practice and experience which country theatres afforded him. Two months later, and Edmund Kean, once more reconciled to Stephen Price, was acting at Drury Lane. His contract with the Covent Garden management had not yet ended, and the proprietors of that theatre accordingly made application to the Court of Chancery to prevent his performing at the other house; but the Lord Chancellor declared he could not interfere in the matter, and it was therefore allowed to rest.

CHAPTER VII.

A new sensation in the theatrical world—The fate of Covent Garden—Fanny Kemble studies Juliet—In an empty theatre—Preparing for a first appearance—A memorable cast—Feelings of the new Juliet—Facing a crowded house—A blissful girl—Wonderful success and its results—An uncomely Romeo—In the provinces—Kean prepares to act Henry V.—Illness and postponement of the play—A pitiful sight—A melancholy letter—Fight for me—At the Victoria Theatre—A remarkable speech—Preparing to visit America once more—A memorable performance.

AT this time a new sensation occurred in the theatrical world. In the year 1822 Charles Kemble, who had been presented by his brother John with a share in Covent Garden Theatre, became desirous of obtaining sway over the management. Henry Harris, manager, and proprietor of seven-twelfths of the theatre, strongly objected to this design, but after much negotiation, treaty, and discussion, a settlement was eventually arrived at, whereby a lease of the whole concern was granted to a trustee, William Harrison, who underlet the premises to Messrs. Kemble, Willett, and Forbes at a rental of twelve thousand a year; not with the intention of receiving profit, but for the purpose of giving the direction and control of the theatre to Messrs. Kemble, Willett, and Forbes; for a stipulation was added, that they were to pay all charges and expenses of the house, and that such profit as might be received should be paid to the trustee, in order that out of that fund the heavy debts due from the concern might be liquidated. Henry Harris then withdrew, and Messrs. Kemble, Willett, and Forbes directed the fortunes of the theatre.

A system of gross mismanagement then set in, and during the course of six years the house was burdened by a debt amounting to almost twenty-three thousand pounds. Charles Kemble was now sadly convinced of the mistake he had made. The prospect stretching before him and his family was assuredly dark, and apparently afforded no room for hope. In August, 1829, whilst he was fulfilling provincial engagements, a warrant of distraint was issued for eight hundred and ninety-six pounds for parish rates and taxes due by the theatre, which was accordingly seized on and advertised for sale.

Returning from a brief walk one day, Mrs. Charles Kemble came into the room where her daughter Fanny, then a girl of nineteen, was sitting, and throwing herself into a chair burst into tears. Startled and grieved at this, Fanny Kemble begged to know what had happened, on which the poor woman answered between her sobs, "Oh, it has come at last—our property is to be sold. I have seen the building all covered with placards and bills, and I know not how many hundred poor people will be turned adrift without employment." The girl strove to comfort her mother by expressions of sympathy and affection, the while a resolution was shaping itself in her mind.

Soon after she retired to her own room, and then wrote a letter to her father requesting he would allow her to become a governess, and so relieve him of the burden of her maintenance. With this in her hand she sought her mother, and asked permission to forward it, which was granted. Next day Mrs. Kemble, who had been an actress of fair repute, inquired of her daughter if she thought she possessed any real talent for the stage, to which the latter replied she did not know whether she did or not. Her mother then told her to learn a part from one of Shakespeare's plays, and recite it, that she might judge the effects. Accordingly Fanny Kemble committed Portia's lines to memory, and having spoken them, was told there was not sufficient passion in the part to test any tragic power she might possess.

To this statement was added a suggestion that she might learn Juliet's speeches, a hint with which the girl readily complied.

In the interim several persons of rank and wealth, thinking it a pity the magnificent wardrobe, fine scenery, and costly decorations of Covent Garden Theatre should be dispersed by auction, liberally subscribed towards paying some portion of the debts. In this effort they were aided by the voluntary offerings of several of the performers, who expected to profit by the re-opening of the house. Moreover, the King's Theatre gave a performance for the benefit of the lessees, which produced seven hundred and fifty pounds; and Miss Foote and Miss Kelly offered to act for ten nights gratuitously, T. P. Cooke for six, and Edmund Kean for three nights, in order to help the lessees.

In September Charles Kemble returned home to face the ruin his directorship had helped to cause; he had not answered his daughter's letter, and she was sorely wondering what her future fate might be, when one evening she was asked by her mother to recite Juliet's speeches to them. It therefore happened, that with anxious mind and fluttering heart she stood before these gentle critics in the great drawing-room of their house in St. James's Street, the blaze of a wood fire and the lustre of wax candles lighting her wistful girlish face and graceful figure, clad in clinging robes of white muslin; they gazing on her with affectionate eyes, and encouraging her with gentle words. And having gone through the various scenes of this passionate romance, until the maiden is done to death by love, Fanny Kemble was assured her efforts were "very nice, my dear," and being kissed and caressed was sent to bed. When halfway up the stairs leading to her room, she sat down, and, overcome by the nervous excitement she had long striven to suppress, burst into tears, and with swollen eyes laid her head upon her pillow that night.

A few days later her father told her he wished to take her to the theatre, which yet remained closed to the public, and accompanying him at midday she stood, a solitary figure, on the wide, dimly-lighted, silent stage of Covent Garden. Kings, princes, poets, warriors, maidens fair and villains foul that had peopled the boards night after night, were there no more; great roughly-painted scenes of palaces and dungeons, banqueting halls and churches lay one beside the other in strange confusion against the high colourless walls; flights of dark steps, winding passages, and trap-doors showed the exits by which those who had trod their brief hours here had vanished and left no trace; before her lay the wide amphitheatre, with boxes and chandeliers shrouded in holland coverings, and galleries stretching into mysterious space; from the high dust-covered windows came straight shafts of sunshine piercing the pervading gloom, and falling upon the stage in points of yellow light.

As she stood in the centre of the boards, surrounded by an impressive atmosphere of mystery, her father's voice, reaching her from the darkness beyond, bade her recite Juliet's speeches. She complied, and by degrees the music of the words and the force of their feeling seizing possession of her, she acted with a passion and ardour that promised fair success. Though unaware of the fact, a spectator other than her father heard her, an old friend of the family, a man of the world, an amateur actor and theatrical critic, in whose judgment Charles Kemble placed confidence. Hidden in the recesses of a private box he watched her, and as she concluded, prophesied her future fame. It was then settled that she should make her first appearance on the stage in the character of Juliet, when the house opened on the 5th of October, 1829, a date within three weeks of the decision.

Great were the preparations made meanwhile; morning rehearsals were daily gone through; the *débutante* made the acquaintance of her fellow-players, not one of whom she had ever spoken with or seen off the stage, and learned to make her entrances and exits with propriety; while at home grave consultations were held regarding the colour and shape of her costumes. An artistic friend suggested they should be after the fashion of those worn in Verona in mediæval days; but Mrs. Kemble, who was conventional and perhaps commonplace, decided in favour of the white satin ball dress, with short sleeves and a long train, which the Juliets of those days invariably wore. Mrs. Siddons had played the Grecian Daughter in an enormous hoop, and piles of powdered curls, from which sprung a forest of feathers, and her niece's costume for the Veronese maiden could boast of being quite as historically correct.

But the question of finding a suitable robe was less trouble than that of seeking a desirable Romeo. Charles Kemble had played that character to the Juliet of Miss O'Neill, but was now much too old for the part. It was therefore thought his son Henry, a slight, well-shaped, and handsome youth, would look an ideal Romeo, but grave fears were entertained regarding his acting. Personally he entertained a strong dislike to the stage, was wholly unable to assume the faintest approach to sentiment. However, to please his parents he learned the part of Romeo; but at a private rehearsal of the balcony scene, his whole appearance and manner were so ridiculous that Juliet burst into fits of laughter, and his father, throwing down the book, roared in concert with her until the tears ran down his cheeks; whilst the lad, now seeing the painful task was done, clapped his elbows against his sides, hopped about the room, and crowed like a cock by way of expressing his delight.

Romeo was eventually entrusted to a player named Abbott, a man who had formerly been in the army, but was now a respectable though not a brilliant actor. His physique was by no means fascinating, and his age was sufficient for him to have been the new Juliet's father. The cast of the play was otherwise excellent, Charles Kemble playing Mercutio for the first time; Mrs. Kemble, who had retired from the stage upwards of twenty years, for this occasion only, represented the Lady Capulet; Robert Keeley, Peter; and Mrs. Davenport the Nurse.

Whilst the general preparations were being made, Fanny Kemble remained, as she narrates, "absolutely passive in the hands of others, taking no part and not much interest in the matter." The fact of her becoming an actress was not, it is regrettable to state, the result of her love of art, but rather from a sense of duty she owed her parents, and in conformity with their will. "The theatrical profession," she writes, "was utterly distasteful to me, though acting itself, that is, dramatic personation, was not; and every detail of my future vocation, from the preparations behind the scenes to the representations before the curtain, was more or less repugnant to me." Later on, when success crowned her efforts, she wrote to a friend, "My task seems such useless work, that, but for the very useful pecuniary results, I think I would rather make shoes." No true artist this.

As time advanced the town became greatly excited by the assurance that the niece of Mrs. Siddons and of John Kemble was about to make her appearance on the stage. Rumours were afloat regarding her grace and beauty, expectation rose concerning her histrionic power. The date of her appearance was fixed for Monday the 5th of October, 1829. On that day there was no rehearsal, lest the *débutante* should be fatigued. She and her mother drove to the theatre early in the evening, whilst yet the sunshine of an autumn day lingered in the sky; as it shone into the carriage Mrs. Kemble, regarding it as a happy omen, turned to her daughter and said, "Heaven smiles on you, my dear." Arriving at Covent Garden Theatre, Fanny Kemble went to the room allotted her, where three women helped her to dress; and her toilet being made she was placed in a chair, over the back of which her white satin train was carefully arranged. "There I sat," she wrote to a friend, "ready for execution, with the palms of my hands pressed convulsively together, and the tears I in vain endeavoured to suppress welling up into my eyes and brimming slowly over, down my rouged cheeks, upon which my aunt with a smile of pity renewed the colour as often as these heavy drops made unsightly streaks upon it. Once and again my father came to the door, and I heard his anxious, 'How is she?' to which my aunt answered, sending him away with words of comforting cheer."

Meanwhile the theatre had become crowded in every part, and an impatient audience waited to welcome the new Juliet. Many were those present who remembered the first appearance on the same stage of Miss O'Neill, and were ready to make comparisons with this new representative of a favourite character. The first scenes of the tragedy had little interest for the house, and a noisy murmur was kept up whilst the actors went through their parts. At last the moment drew near when Juliet must appear, and the call-boy's brisk rap at her door made her start to her feet. She was then led round to the wings, where she caught sight of her mother going on the stage, and heard the uproar that greeted her appearance.

Filled with terror, Fanny Kemble lay in her aunt's arms, waiting for the moment of her entrance, surrounded by half the *dramatis personæ*, all of whom were sympathetic with her fears and anxious for her success.

"Courage, courage, dear child; poor thing, poor thing," murmured kindly old Mrs. Davenport, memories of her first appearance coming dimly back through long years.

"Never mind 'em, Miss Kemble," said Robert Keeley in his comical, nervous, lachrymose voice, "never mind 'em; don't think of 'em any more than if they were so many rows of cabbages."

There was no time for more; the Nurse was called, and she in her turn cried out for Juliet. The long-dreaded moment came. "My aunt," says Fanny Kemble, "gave me an impulse forward, and I ran straight across the stage, stunned with the tremendous shout that greeted me, my eyes covered with mist, and the green baize flooring of the stage feeling as if it rose up against my feet; but I got hold of my mother, and stood like a terrified creature at bay, confronting the huge theatre full of gazing human beings. I do not think a word I uttered during the scene could have been audible." At her entrance the whole house burst into a storm—the pit rose, the boxes applauded, the gallery cheered. For some seconds her confusion and nervousness were so great she could not speak, but stood gazing at the scene before her as if fascinated by its tumult, her dark eyes bright with excitement, her delicately curved face paling beneath its rouge, but presently recovering herself, she was enabled to begin her part. Her meeting with Romeo was treated with delicacy and poetry; in owning her love for him she expressed a charm and innocence surpassingly beautiful; and as the influence of "the inauspicious stars" which swayed her destiny was felt, and stronger passions were called forth, her acting became powerful, and at points sublime.

The expression of her countenance, the inflection of her voice, the grace of her movements occasionally recalled memories of Mrs. Siddons, and frequently she was interrupted by applause which her fine elocution and picturesque attitudes elicited. In the balcony scene all self-consciousness had disappeared, "and for aught

I know," she narrates, "I was Juliet; the passion I was uttering sending hot waves of blushes all over my neck and shoulders, while the poetry sounded like music to me as I spoke it, with no consciousness of anything before me, utterly transported into the imaginary existence of the play." At the fall of the curtain the house rang with cheers, and on Charles Kemble coming forward, he returned thanks to the audience for the reception given his daughter, and stated the tragedy would be performed on the following Wednesday, Friday, and Monday, an announcement that was received with enthusiasm. But though her success was undoubted, it is not certain she was quite happy; for speaking of this evening years later, she says she never presented herself before an audience without a shrinking feeling of reluctance, or withdrawn from their presence without thinking the excitement she had undergone unhealthy, and the personal exhibition odious. "Nevertheless," she adds, "I sat me down to supper that night with my poor rejoicing parents, well content, God knows, with the issue of my trial; and still better pleased with a lovely little Geneva watch, the first I had ever possessed, all encrusted with gold work and jewels, which my father laid by my plate, and I immediately christened Romeo, and went, a blissful girl, to sleep with it under my pillow."

Romeo and Juliet continued to be played three times weekly from October to December, when Fanny Kemble appeared as Belvidira in *Venice Preserved*. She was universally lauded by the town, but so much could not be said for the elderly Romeo, Abbott. He indeed became an object of special aversion to the youthful and enthusiastic crowd of Juliet's admirers, who nightly gathered in the pit to worship her and envy him. Nor was poor Abbott left long in ignorance of his utter unfitness for the part he played; for it happened that three of Juliet's devoted adherents, when walking home towards Cavendish Square one night after the performance, fell to abusing Romeo with great zest, unmercifully dwelling on his uncouth gestures, his unmusical voice, his vague expression, the fullness of his years, giving moreover burlesque imitations of his acting, much to their own satisfaction. The hour being late the streets were deserted and silent, and every word they spoke fell with terrible distinctness on the ears of a solitary figure that preceded them by a few yards. Suddenly this individual halted at a gas-lamp, and turning round, faced the youths, who with horror and remorse recognized the well-known features of Abbott. There they stood, still and wordless from surprise.

"Gentlemen," said the actor calmly, "no one can be better aware than myself of the defects of my performance of Romeo, no one more conscious of its entire unworthiness of Miss Kemble's Juliet; but all I can say is, that I don't act the part by my own choice, and shall be delighted to resign it to whichever of you finds himself more capable than I am of doing it justice." Saying which he bowed, and vanished before they could recover their astonishment or speak a word of apology.

Fanny Kemble now became a popular idol. Sir Thomas Laurence a few days before his death had made a sketch of her as Juliet, engravings from which were exhibited in the shop-windows; saucers, plates, and jugs bore her likeness; men of fashion wore portraits of her in the characters of Juliet and Belvidira stamped on their neck-handkerchiefs; the press lauded her daily; the theatre was crowded by enthusiastic audiences whenever she played, and her name was on all men's lips. To her the reward of success was pleasant; instead of having an allowance of twenty pounds from her father, out of which she was obliged to provide herself with many articles necessary to her toilet, she had now a salary of thirty guineas a week from Covent Garden, with prospects of far more remunerative engagements in the provinces; instead of trudging through the muddy London streets when the hire of a hackney coach was a serious consideration, she had a handsome carriage; she took riding lessons, and bought a horse for herself and another for her father; in place of wearing threadbare, faded, or dyed, and turned gowns, she had fashionably-made dresses, in which she looked transfigured. Moreover, her company was eagerly sought by the world of fashion and distinction; visitors came in numbers to her father's door, deep interest was felt in her career, and a brilliant prospect prophesied for her by all who approached her. But perhaps the most gratifying fact in connection with this eventful period was, that through her success the management of the theatre was at the close of the season enabled to pay its creditors thirteen thousand pounds.

In the summer she visited Bath, Glasgow, Liverpool, Edinburgh, and Dublin. The playgoers of the first-mentioned town were much less enthusiastic than the Covent Garden audiences; whilst the staid and sober people of Glasgow were absolutely cold, and the death-stillness which succeeded her outbursts chilled the heart of the young actress. Her reception at Edinburgh was not less depressing. Mrs. Siddons had in days gone by regarded her performances before the people of the Scottish capital as dreaded ordeals, and seeing their stolidity after those great efforts, which were wont to rouse audiences in every other town in the kingdom to the highest pitch of enthusiasm, would pant out in despair, "Oh, stupid people; oh, stupid people!" Stupid they were not, but cold and hard to move; yet the triumph of stirring them was at last given to this gifted woman, for on one occasion when she played Lady Macbeth to them, the sleep-walking scene was encored, and had to be repeated before they permitted the tragedy to proceed.

At Liverpool Fanny Kemble acted to more appreciative houses; whilst in Dublin she met the kindliest and warmest greeting. The first night of her appearance at the Theatre Royal was memorable. The house was crowded by a brilliant audience, which included the most distinguished men and women of the capital; she was greeted with rapture, and applauded with fervour, her youth, grace, and beauty making her an immediate favourite with a highly sensitive people. On leaving the house she was escorted to her hotel by a bodyguard of over two hundred strong, "shouting and hurraying like mad." When the carriage arrived at its destination a rush was made to let down the steps, and hand the young actress out. Then the crowd formed a line for her to pass through their ranks, many of them dropping on their knees to look under her bonnet, as she ran laughing with her head down from the carriage to the house; and as she disappeared they gave her three ringing cheers.

On the second night of her performance a crowd again gathered round the stage door; and on her father coming out, cheers were given for "Misther Charles;" and he being followed by a lady they mistook for his wife, cheers were also given for "Misthress Charles;" and once again three ringing cheers were given for Miss Fanny.

"An' sure it's herself looks well by gaslight," said one of the bystanders. "Aye, and bedad she looks well by daylight too," adds another; and away the carriage started, with a light-hearted crowd in its wake, hurraying right merrily; and in this way the Irish capital showed its appreciation for beauty and talent. One day, whilst walking up Sackville Street, Charles Kemble experienced a specimen of Hibernian flattery and subtlety worth recording. Two ancient dames, beggars, whose profession had evidently been brought to highest perfection by constant practice, followed him. "Och, but he's an illigant man entirely is Misther Charles Kemble," said one of the crones in a stage whisper. "'Deed, so was his brother, Misther John," replied her companion, in the same key, "a mighty fine man; an' t' see his demanour puttin' his hand in his pocket to give me sixpence, bate all the world."

Whilst Fanny Kemble drew crowds to Covent Garden during her first season, Kean played a round of his old characters at Drury Lane, and presently became desirous of appearing in some part in which the public had not previously seen him. It was much feared his power of memory had failed because he had been unable to retain the lines of *Ben Nazir;* but since then he had played *Virginius* for the first time at Covent Garden with success; from which it was argued his mind had recovered its vigour. Accordingly, he now resolved to represent the king in Shakespeare's play of *Henry V.* Great preparations were made for the event; Kean studied his part resolutely, the characters were carefully cast, new scenery was painted, and frequent rehearsals took place.

At last *Henry V.* was announced for performance on the 22nd of February, 1830; but on the evening of that day, whilst dressing for his part, Kean was seized by an attack that produced great lassitude and complete stupor. His dresser immediately shouted for help, and the manager arriving, found the poor player unable to recognize him; his face haggard and ghastly under the glaring rouge, his limbs clad in regal garments, motionless, as if stretched in death—a pitiful sight of a human life foundered in the zenith of its days.

Fortunately the doors of the theatre had not yet been opened, and a notice was immediately posted on them announcing Kean's illness, and the delay of the representation of *Henry V.* The prostration from which the tragedian suffered was not unusual, with some care he rallied; therefore on the 8th of March he was again advertised for the part of the king. On this evening a great audience filled the house, and expectation rose. At the usual hour the orchestra began an overture, at the conclusion of which the curtain remained down, and an awkward pause ensued. After a while music was again played, but when it ceased the curtain still remained lowered. The audience now became fearful lest something had gone wrong; and their apprehensions were much increased by hearing the overture once more. Noise and confusion followed, which was only quelled by the rising of the curtain.

Then the play began. In the second scene, Kean

as Henry V. was discovered, splendidly dressed in robes of crimson and purple velvet adorned with gold, seated on a throne, and surrounded by his court. Loud applause greeted him, followed by breathless silence, when he began his part, spoke two or three lines, hesitated, paused, waited for the prompter's aid, continued a few words, added, skipped, and mangled the text. The audience looked on with amazement, consternation, and regret. Here was a great actor, such as perhaps the English stage had not seen, one who a few years since had power to raise the emotions of his hearers to the highest pitch, now a miserable wreck in mind and body—an object of pity to the charitable, of scorn to the scoffer, ruined by his own deeds. The curtain fell in silence.

Between the first and second acts a long pause ensued, but the house, believing their old favourite was striving to recover himself, bore the delay with patience; they were not, however, rewarded by any improvement in his acting. One fourth of what was set down for him in the second act was not spoken, and the other actors, thrown completely out, were obliged to curtail their speeches in an attempt to make them join in some coherent manner. About the middle of the third act the well-tested forbearance of the audience gave way, and hisses were heard, but no notice was taken of them by Kean. An interval of half an hour followed between the fourth and fifth acts, and this completely destroyed whatever patience the house had heretofore exercised. Hissing, hooting, and cries for the manager followed, and the general clamour by no means ceased when the curtain rose. Not a word spoken in the first scene was heard; in the second Kean made his entrance, but his voice was also drowned by the tumult. For a moment he stood anxious, bewildered, and undecided, then advanced to the front of the stage, and baring his head, intimated his desire to address the house.

For several minutes he was unable to obtain silence, but when this was granted him, he said in a trembling, uncertain voice, "Ladies and Gentlemen, it is now many years since I have had the honour to enjoy a large share of your approbation. You may conceive, therefore, how deeply I deplore this moment when for the first time I incur your displeasure." (Cries of "No, no, not the first time.") "If you wish that I should proceed," he answered, drawing himself up, "I must request your silence. For many years, give me leave to say, I have worked hard for your entertainment." ("You have been well paid for it," interrupted a voice, of which he took no heed.) "That very labour and the lapse of time and circumstances have no doubt had their effects upon my mind." ("Why do you drink so hard?" a voice of brutal candour inquired.) Poor Kean paused and hesitated; the cup of his humiliation was now full, and it was with a struggle he continued, "Ladies and Gentlemen, I feel that I stand before you in a most degraded situation." (Shouts of " No, no," and " Why did you put yourself into it?") "You are my countrymen, and I appeal with confidence to that liberality which has always distinguished Englishmen." And putting his hand upon his heart he bowed, and retiring to his place amongst the other performers, continued the scene. The few speeches that remained for him to make were again mangled and abbreviated, so that the whole act did not occupy ten minutes, and the play concluded amidst expressions of disapproval and general tumult. Two days later Kean wrote the following letter, the characters of which are traced with a trembling and uncertain hand. It bears no address, but presumably is written to the manager of Drury Lane Theatre.

"*March* 10, 1830.

"I address you, sir, under the most painful feelings that human nature can endure—a loss of that by which I lived, the public favour, and my only hope. My only consolation in this extreme of misery is, that it was neither from want of attention to my duties nor want of recollection of their former kindness. It is that kindness that too much dazzled me. It was that that brought me to superhuman calculations, and favoured by the approbation of the public, I conceived myself invulnerable. Mind cannot be directed, as I have proved in this last most destructive issue. But want of memory is not want of heart, and while a pulsation is left, it beats with gratitude and affection to that public who brought me from obscurity into a light I never dreamt of, and it overpowered me. I find too late that I must rest upon my former favours. My heart is willing, but my memory has flown. All that I have done I can and will; what is to do I leave to a rising generation. Kindness and urbanity will remember how long and zealously I have made my grateful bow to the British public, living on their smiles, destroyed by their censure, both of which I have comparatively deserved. Let me once more have to say, that the old spoiled favourite is forgiven; let me once more pursue that path which led me to your favour, and die in grateful recollection of the debt I owe to a sympathizing though sometimes an unjustly angry public."

He also wrote to his friend W. H. Halpin, the editor of the *Star* newspaper, the following pitiful note—

"DEAR HALPIN,

"Fight for me, I have no resources in myself; mind is gone, and body is hopeless. God knows my heart. I would do, but cannot. Memory, the first of goddesses, has forsaken me, and I am left without a hope but from those old resources that the public and myself are tired of. Damn, God damn ambition. The soul leaps, the body falls.

"EDMUND KEAN."

Halpin felt compassion for him, and criticizing his performance of *Henry V.* says, "Owing to the indisposition of this favourite and popular performer, the attempt proved a decided failure. The want of his usual energy, and his incorrectness in the delivery of the text, excited the disapprobation of the audience, so far as rendered it necessary for him to make an apology."

In a few days Kean is able to inform Halpin that he is "reinstated in all his dignities and privileges, and can write as usual;" for his engagement at Drury Lane was continued, and on the 15th of the month he played Richard III. with something of his old spirit, and was warmly received and heartily applauded. "To us," says a morning paper, "it is a matter of doubt if he ever played Richard better than on Monday. It does credit to his feelings to record his agitation before he began. He felt that he had offended the public, and the fear of meeting their displeasure almost convulsed his frame. Perspiration rolled down his cheeks, and his nerves would have completely failed him had he not experienced so kind a reception. He recovered his self-possession instantly, and, Antæus-like, rose unhurt by his fall. His exclamation, 'Richard's himself again,' was heartily cheered by the audience, a compliment which he seemed to feel deeply. His basilisk glance at the young prince was absolutely withering, and forcibly reminded us of John Kemble's answer to a friend who asked him what was Kean's greatest recommendation—'His eye, look at his eye, sir.'"

On that day week he played Hamlet, a character he had not represented for upwards of four years. From the vigour with which he went through the first act, it was believed his health was much better than usual; but occasional inaccuracies and transpositions in the delivery of the text, together with omissions, were observable; and points which had roused enthusiasm before, now missed their mark. The failure of his powers was sad to behold; but to those behind the curtain it was far more observable than to his audience. During those scenes of the play in which he did not appear on the stage, he sat at the wings, being too fatigued for the passage to his dressing-room, or to the green-room, panting, flushed, and exhausted by the efforts he had just made, his dresser standing beside him with a glass of hot brandy punch, which the tragedian drank to sustain his energies during the next scene. He was now able to play but once a week, and would have wholly rested, but that he depended for support on the fifty pounds a night he invariably received for his representations.

The offer of a hundred pounds for two nights' performances on one occasion induced him to act at the Victoria Theatre. On the first night of his appearance at this house he acted Richard III. to a large and delighted audience, whose enthusiasm was all he could desire; but on the second evening, when he played Othello to the Iago of Cobham, an old Victorian favourite, his reception was not so flattering. The crowd was as great as on the former occasion, but more noisy and less attentive. Kean's speeches were frequently interrupted or freely commented on, as was the prevailing fashion of this house; the popping of ginger-beer bottles in the gallery marred his best effects, and, above all, he was continually irritated by cries of "Bravo, Cobham, bravo!" the applause he received being much less than that given to Cobham. At this want of judgment Kean's indignation, which had been inflamed by liberal potions of brandy-and-water, overflowed, and when called before the curtain at the close of the tragedy, he hesitated to obey. But the clamour continuing, he walked forward to the centre of the stage, his eyes flashing with anger, the paint but half rubbed from his cheeks, a cloak wrapped round him, and abruptly demanded, "What do you want?" This question, so suddenly asked, caused momentary surprise, but soon a volley of voices shouted in reply, "You, you, you." "Well, then, here I am," answered Kean. "I have acted in every theatre in the United Kingdom of Great Britain and Ireland, and in all the principal towns throughout the United States of America, but in my life I never acted to such a set of ignorant, unmitigated brutes as I now see before me;" saying which, he flung a corner of his cloak over one shoulder, and slowly made his exit.

The manager and his company, who had crowded to the wings in order to listen to this unrehearsed speech, could scarce believe they heard aright, and now expected the house would be torn down and left a blackened ruin, to mark the indignation of the offended gods. A frightful silence, such as precedes the roaring of thunder, followed, when suddenly a voice called out, "Cobham, Cobham," a cry that was taken up and repeated until the theatre shook; a show of enthusiasm for their old favourite being considered the best way of punishing the great actor. Cobham appeared bowing and smiling, and went through pantomimical expressions of gratitude and emotion, until silence was granted, when he said, "Ladies and Gentlemen, this is unquestionably the proudest moment of my life. I cannot give utterance to my feelings; but to the latest hour of my existence I shall cherish the remembrance of the honour conferred upon me by one of the most distinguished, liberal, and enlightened audiences I ever had the pleasure of addressing." The cheers which filled the house at the conclusion of his speech were loud and lusty, and Cobham withdrew, greatly gratified by an ovation which still more mortified Kean.

In June and July (1830) the great tragedian played Richard III., Shylock, Sir Giles Overreach, and King Lear at the Haymarket, the same theatre in which twenty-four years ago he had acted most subordinate parts. Between that time and this his life had been singularly full of events; bitter struggles had been crowned by brilliant victory; the world had smiled and frowned upon him; health, reputation, and wealth had been given him, and he had squandered them wantonly; and now it seemed as if his existence must end in darkness and despair.

A desire at this time beset him to return once more to America, where his performances had proved so remunerative; and being slow to perceive, or loath to acknowledge, the great changes which had taken place in him, he believed the same results would follow another visit to the States. Accordingly, it was advertised that he would take his farewell benefit previous to his departure for New York at the King's Theatre—now known as Her Majesty's—on the 19th of July, when he would perform an act of each of the great plays in which he had made his fame. This announcement caused great excitement, and drew an enormous concourse of people round the doors of the theatre as early as four o'clock in the afternoon.

With every minute the crowd increased, and eventually overflowed the arcade, and extended far down the street. At half-past five those in the centre of the throng, becoming afraid of being suffocated, called for the opening of the doors, but in vain; escape was found impossible by those immured in the centre of the dense mass, and the pressure became unendurable. Women screamed and fainted; an effort was made to force the entrances; in vexation the people broke the windows, and the glasses of lamps within reach. At last the doors were thrown open, and a terrific rush followed. In a few moments not only every available seat in the immense pit and gallery was taken, but the box tiers, lobbies, and stairs were crowded. To afford greater accommodation, the whole of the space usually occupied by the orchestra was given up to the people, whilst presently the wings of the stage became so overcrowded with spectators, that it was impossible for them to keep out of sight of the body of the house.

It was estimated that the receipts amounted to a thousand pounds. Many had come under the belief that this was the last time they would ever have an opportunity of seeing Edmund Kean play; and to his numerous admirers the occasion was one in which sadness was mingled with pleasure. The performance was advertised to consist of the fourth acts of *Richard III.* and *The Merchant of Venice*, the fifth act of *A New Way* to *Pay Old Debts*, the second act of *Macbeth*, and the third act of *Othello*.

For an hour the dense mass of closely-packed people waited patiently till the curtain rose. An orchestra arranged upon the stage played the overture, at the conclusion of which the curtain was dropped to prepare for the performance. When it was again raised, Kean was discovered as Richard III., dressed in royal robes, and seated on a throne. The cheers that rose were loud and ringing, in the midst of which he, with regal dignity, descended the daïs, advanced to the front of the stage, and bowed repeatedly.

The act then began, but was frequently interrupted by the disputes and noise caused by the overcrowding, as well as from the angry shouts of those in the gallery to the people forced by pressure on to the stage from the side scenes. Kean, who had evidently reserved his strength for this trying occasion, at first acted with vigour, his step seeming more firm than usual, his voice sounding strong and clear. His representation of Othello recalled pleasant memories of his earlier days, and as Shylock he was excellent; but his playing of Sir Giles Overreach was unimpressive; whilst as Macbeth his memory failed him on several occasions. At the conclusion, the clamour of an excited audience, suppressed throughout the performance, broke out. Loud applause and cries for Kean sounded from all parts of the house, in response to which he, dressed in the character of the Moor, was led forward by one of the players. His appearance increased the enthusiasm; wreaths were flung upon the stage, those who had stood at the wings crowded round him, and it was quite five minutes before silence could be obtained; then he spoke with much feeling, saying—

"Ladies and Gentlemen, I hope that none of you can understand the pain and agitation which fills my heart at this climax of my career, or the acute suffering I endure now that I am about to quit the country that has given me birth, and the people whom I have adored, to visit a land where perhaps nothing but ill-health and sorrow await me. I feel it quite impossible to express my gratitude for the constant ebullitions of your approbation which you have this night and always bestowed upon me. For the favour and popularity I have always enjoyed, the fact of performing in one night all my favourite characters was the best, the only return my gratitude could make you. I will not particularly allude to past or to future events, but now that I am about to leave you for ever, most earnestly from my heart I entreat that you will suffer no empirics to usurp the dramatic throne, to the ruin and disgrace of the drama. I must and will venture to assert, that the well-being of the stage is of the utmost consequence to a nation's morality. Ladies and gentlemen, the time has now arrived for me to return you all my most fervent thanks, and to bid you a long, a last farewell." The applause which followed was loud and fervid, and the audience left the theatre with the impression that they had seen the last of a great and favourite actor.

CHAPTER VIII.

Robert William Elliston becomes lessee of the Surrey Theatre—Whimsical speeches to his audiences—Douglas Jerrold and his plays—Little Shakespeare in a camlet cloak—First production of *Black-Eyed Susan*—Elliston's last days—Charles Young says farewell to the public—Fanny Kemble bids good-bye to England—Charles Kean's struggles—Visit to America—Junius Brutus Booth at Orleans—Playing at Boston — Strange incident — His exit from life's stage—Edmund Kean at Richmond—Failing health—Helen Faucit's Recollections of him—His last performance—Reconciliation with his wife—His last days and his death.

FROM 1830 to 1833 some memorable events occurred in theatrical annals. Robert William Elliston on leaving Drury Lane became for the second time lessee of the Surrey Theatre, having paid eight hundred and seventy pounds before being allowed to take possession of the house. He then refitted the interior, made many improvements in the building, and gathered a competent company under his banner. The house was opened on Whit Monday, 1827, on which occasion the manager made one of his characteristic speeches.

All his energies and much of his vivacity were exercised in catering for the Surrey audiences, and occasionally his resources were tasked in striving to soothe and divert them. His tact, however, was unfailing. One evening during the performance of a serious drama, a sailor in the gallery, who was elevated in more senses than one, continually interrupted the progress of the play by sundry remarks, shouted at the pitch of his voice, and various comments addressed to his neighbours, much to their annoyance. Recriminations and threats followed, and by degrees the audience became much disturbed, when Elliston came forward and said—

"May I know the cause of this unseemly clamour?"

"It's this here sailor what makes the row," cried a voice from the gallery.

"A British sailor," said Elliston, "the glory of our country's annals, the safeguard of our homes and families. What is it he asks?"

"*Rule Britannia*," shouted the tar.

"You shall have it," answered the manager decisively. "Of what ship, comrade?"

"The *Haggermemnon*," replied the sailor.

"Ladies and Gentlemen," said Elliston in a serious tone, as he addressed the house. "On Monday next a nautical, national, allegorical sketch will be performed in the theatre, entitled *The British Flag*, in which the whole strength of the company will be employed; the music expressly composed by Mr. Blewitt. Give 'em *Rule Britannia*," he added to the musicians, and raising his head towards the gallery, said to the sailor, "Bring your companions here on Monday," and then made his exit. *Rule Britannia* was sung by the company, and the play allowed to proceed without further interruption. The nautical, national, allegorical sketch he had promised was never performed, it having no existence save in the manager's eccentric brain.

A few weeks later, when another play was rendered inaudible because of the confusion which followed on overcrowding, Elliston again came forward to soothe or to cajole his patrons.

"I take the liberty of addressing you, ladies and gentlemen," he said, in his most solemn manner. "It is of rare occurrence that I deem it necessary to place myself in juxtaposition with you." (Noise in the gallery.) "When I said juxtaposition I meant *vis-à-vis*" (increased noise in the gallery); "when I uttered the words *vis-à-vis* I meant contactability. Now let me tell you that *vis-à-vis* (it is a French term) and contactability (which is a truly English term) very nearly assimilate each other." (Here the disturbance became general.) "Gentlemen, gentlemen, I am really ashamed of your conduct. It is unlike a Surrey audience. Are you aware that I have in this establishment most efficient peace officers at my immediate disposal? Peace officers, gentlemen, mean persons necessary in time of war." (He strode towards the wings, hesitated, and again advanced.) "One word more," he continued. "If that tall gentleman in the carpenter's cap will sit down" (here he pointed to the pit), "the little girl behind him in red ribbons—you, my love, I mean," he said, addressing himself to an imaginary child—" will be able to see the entertainment." Bowing elaborately he made his exit, and the house, satisfied by his speech, settled into silence.

Fortune now smiled on his endeavours, so that in 1830 he was not only able to return money lent him, furnish his house in Great Surrey Street at a cost of five hundred pounds, and live at ease, but likewise place the sum of two thousand pounds in the three per cents.

In accumulating this amount he was largely aided by the production of the great nautical drama *Black-Eyed Susan, or All in the Downs*. It happened one day that Elliston received a visit from Douglas Jerrold, then a young struggling journalist and playwright, entirely depending on his pen, not only for his own support, but for that of those dearer to him than life. Though but in his twenty-sixth year, Douglas Jerrold had written many dramas, brimful of humour, and tender because human, most of which are now forgotten, amongst them being *The Living Skeleton, Sally in our Alley, Ambrose Gwinnett, Fifteen Years of a Drunkard's Life, The Flying Dutchman,* &c., so that he was known amongst his associates as "Little Shakespeare in the camlet cloak."

Previous to his visiting Elliston he had quarrelled with Davidge, once a harlequin, and subsequently manager of the Coburg or Victoria Theatre, where many of Jerrold's pieces had been produced. Davidge was a ruthless, remorseless taskmaster, who ground the struggling author to the dust, until at last he parted from him in anger. Elliston, therefore, knew the playwright by reputation, and with his usual acuteness foreseeing his worth, was willing to secure it at the lowest price possible. Accordingly, before they parted he engaged Douglas Jerrold as dramatic writer to his establishment at a salary of five pounds a week. The bargain being completed, Douglas Jerrold took from under his camlet cloak the manuscript of *Black-Eyed Susan,* and left it with the manager.

The drama was read, put in rehearsal, and produced

for the first time on Whit-Monday, June 8th, 1829, T. P. Cooke playing the part of William. The audience assembled in the little theatre on this warm evening were noisy, and scarce attentive. Now and then, when they grasped the wit of a sentence, they roared with laughter, though their interest in Susan's unhappy situation was insufficient to stay their clamour. But presently, just previous to the execution of the gallant tar, when the captain enters and proves William to have been discharged previous to striking his officer, the incident had an electric effect upon them, so that, understanding the situation, they burst into enthusiastic applause.

For the first half-dozen nights, however, the drama, though fairly applauded, gave no promise of the extraordinary popularity it subsequently attained; but in the second week of its representation it grew rapidly in favour, and not only were the pit and gallery crowded nightly, but the boxes, usually vacant, were now regularly packed with spectators, who had evidently come from the west. "All London," we are told, "went over the water, and Cooke became a personage in society as Garrick had been in the days of Goodman's Fields." Evening after evening the house was filled; tears were shed over the woes of Susan, laughter pealed over the sayings of the gardener, and the treasury grew heavy.

On the three hundredth night of the representation, Elliston had the exterior of the theatre illuminated; great crowds thronged the street, and it seemed as if a national holiday was being celebrated. But whilst testimonials were raised to mark its success, and presented to Elliston and Cooke, the poor author felt little benefit from his popularity, receiving only about seventy pounds as his share of the profits.

"My dear boy," the florid, fluent manager said to him, "why don't you get your friends to present you with a piece of plate?" That Elliston himself should give the young author some memento of the occasion never entered his head.

"Ah," said a friend to Douglas Jerrold, "you'll be the Surrey Shakespeare."

"The sorry Shakespeare, you mean," replied the dramatist sadly.

It is also worthy of remark, that a considerable sum was also brought into Elliston's treasury by the production of an opera called *Sylvanna*, which was the first musical composition of Carl Maria von Weber performed in England.

It was noticeable towards the end of the year 1830,

that Elliston, who had by no means led a regular or a temperate life, began to show unmistakable signs of decay. Suddenly it seemed as if the airy lightness of his step had given place to a slower and heavier pace, the fullness of his voice to a thinner treble, and his characteristic vivacity to occasional despondency. Rest from exertion and abstinence from drink partially restored him, but the strength he husbanded in this way was ruthlessly spent in conviviality; and early in 1831, it was plainly perceptible to all that his days in the land would be of short duration.

That he was aware of this was probable, for it happened one day a distant connection of his called on him, and having passed an hour in pleasant discourse was about to depart, when Elliston begged he would outstay some other visitors present, as he had something in particular to communicate. And presently, those referred to having taken their leave, Elliston, turning to his relative in a serious and emphatic voice, said, that the night before he had a mysterious warning, and was quite convinced his last days were at hand. "I am," he continued, "prepared for the event, and should it come in the immediate way of the strange warning I have received, I shall die contented."

But again he rallied, and once more appeared upon

the stage on the 24th of June, but to all present his performance was that of a dying man, and it was with evident difficulty he was enabled to finish his part. Before the play concluded he had been announced to act again on the 28th, but when that date arrived it was stated that illness prevented his appearance.

On Wednesday, the 6th of July, 1831, he was seized with an apoplectic fit, and lingered till the following Friday, when the curtain fell upon his life, in the fifty-sixth year of his age. His remains were laid in a vault of St. John's Church, Waterloo Road, and on the south side of the altar a marble tablet bearing a Latin inscription was erected to his memory.

In a brief paper Charles Lamb has immortalized the name of the sometime merry player and ambitious manager. His words are fine gold—" Great wert thou in thy life, Robert William Elliston; and not lessened in thy death, if report speaks truly, which says that thou didst direct that thy mortal remains should repose under no inscription save that of pure Latinity. For thee the Pauline Muses weep! In elegies that shall silence this rude prose, they shall celebrate thy praise."

In the merry month of May in the following year, Charles Young, whom Byron described as the "quintessence of mediocrity," retired from the stage. He selected for his farewell performance the tragedy of *Hamlet*, the same in which he had made his first bow to a London public at the Haymarket Theatre five-and-twenty years before. Charles Mathews, who had on that occasion played Polonius, likewise represented it now, whilst Macready played the Ghost. When Charles Young was asked why he decided on quitting the stage whilst yet in the vigour of life and strength of his powers, he sagely replied, it was better he retired whilst in the enjoyment of public favour, than wait until in the process of time he lost such esteem as he then possessed. A man of regular habits and temperate life, he had amassed a sufficient sum to live at ease for the remainder of his days, and loving quietude, he sought retirement.

On the evening of the 30th of May, 1832, Covent Garden Theatre was crowded to witness his farewell performance; the house was closely packed, and the audience feeling uncomfortable, great confusion arose, so that during the first scene of the tragedy the players' voices were completely drowned, and for some time they continued their parts in pantomime. At last Young appeared, when he hoped the audience would become attentive, but in this he was mistaken, for those who suffered from over-crowding were anxious to vent their wrongs. Young then advanced to the front of the stage, and expressed his regret that more persons had been admitted than the house could accommodate, and promised their money should be returned to all "who would have the kindness to take it and quit the theatre." None, however, seemed anxious to seize advantage of the offer, and after a while the clamour subsided, and the play was heard without interruption save that of applause. Being called for at the conclusion, he said in his farewell speech he had often stood before them with a fluttering heart and a faltering tongue, but never till then with a sense of pain and a degree of heaviness which almost stilled the beating of the one and impeded the utterance of the other. He would fain have been spared the task, but had he not complied with this long-established usage, he should have laid himself open to the charge of lacking respect for his patrons. He proudly acknowledged the indulgence and kindness they had shown him for five-and-twenty years, and he was cheered to find himself still supported by their approbation and presence. Although retirement from the stage and from the excitement of his profession had long been his fervent wish, yet there were feelings and associations connected with the theatre, and with the boards on which he stood, that made him despair of finding words to express his gratitude. He surely spoke no more than truth when he stated, that whatever of good name and of fortune he had obtained, or whatever worldly ambition he had gratified, were due to the public.

"It has been asked," he concluded, "why I retire from the stage while still in possession of whatever qualifications I could ever pretend to unimpaired. I will give you my notions, although I do not know you will accept them as reasons; but reason and feeling are not always cater-cousins. I feel, then, the toil and excitement of my calling weigh more heavily upon me than formerly; and if my qualifications are unimpaired, so would I have them remain in your estimate. I know that they were never worthy of the approbation with which you honoured them; but such as they are, I am loath to remain before my patrons until I have nothing better to present to them than tarnished metal. Permit me then to hope, that on quitting this spot I am honourably dismissed into private life, and that I shall carry with me the kind wishes of all to whom I say respectfully and gratefully—Farewell."

Though Fanny Kemble's exertions had stayed the ruined fortunes of Covent Garden Theatre for a while, they were unable wholly to redeem them, and it was finally settled in 1832 that the house should be let to Laporte, a French manager and *entrepreneur*, whilst Charles Kemble with his daughter should visit America for a couple of years, and strive to retrieve his fortunes.

Accordingly, on Friday evening, the 22nd of June, 1832, Fanny Kemble made her farewell appearance in Sheridan Knowles's comedy of *The Hunchback*. And the play being ended, the audience clamoured loudly until the young actress and her father stood before them, when the excitement became greater still. Then with dim eyes she glanced round the familiar house, and at the excited faces turned towards her own; and in her agitation and grief at parting from kind patrons who had become as old friends, she snatched a little nosegay from her sash and flung it into the pit, with handfuls of kisses as a good-bye token of the affection and gratitude she felt towards them, and bowing, retired from their sight, whilst their cheers rang in her ears.

And once behind the curtain she sobbed, and the tears she had with difficulty suppressed rolled down her cheeks, as many of those who had acted with her crowded round and grasped her hands, and spoke her words of sympathy and kindness. It was the last time indeed that she was destined to act upon that stage, for the house was entirely burnt down in 1856. In the course of the day before that on which he left London, two writs of arrest were served on Charles Kemble by the creditors of the theatre, so that he feared it would not be possible to take his intended journey, but after much anxiety and vexation he was allowed to depart in peace. Early in September, after a voyage of over thirty days, he and his daughter arrived in New York, and on making their respective public appearances were warmly received, so that their united efforts helped to restore the drama in America to the popularity it had previously lost from want of efficient players.

Whilst these events were taking place Charles Kean still strove to win his way to fame. His struggle was hard, for though his name gained that attention from the public which was denied to men of far greater merit, nature had not endowed him with a high order of talent, and his best efforts caused little admiration. In 1830 he visited Amsterdam and the Hague, as a member of an English company playing under the management of Aubrey. This individual was a penniless adventurer, who tempted his actors abroad with promises of liberal salaries which he never intended paying. Having been unprosperous with his troop at the Hague, he at the end of three weeks was unmannerly enough to disappear without taking leave of his company, whom he left penniless strangers in a strange land. That they might reach England they gave a performance for their general benefit, and the sum realized from this, together with a present sent them by the King of Holland, enabled them to return home.

Charles Kean next resolved to seek his fortune in America, which was even then regarded as an El Dorado by those who had made a name in the mother country. Having no difficulty in obtaining an engagement, he early in September, 1830, made his first appearance in the Park Theatre, New York, in the character of Richard III. The house was crowded by an audience curious to see the son of one who, during his visits to the States, had caused such general attention. His entrance was the signal for a warm welcome, but his acting was weak and unequal; now and then by voice and gesture he recalled his father's excellence, but the memory merely contrasted his own insufficiency, and all who held high expectations of his performance were bitterly disappointed. Managers, believing his name would attract, had eagerly bid for him, and he had stipulated to receive a clear half of each night's gross receipts, besides being paid full price for half the shareholders' free admissions. He therefore benefited financially, but the treasury of the theatres at which he played reaped little advantage from his visits. On making his first appearance in the Adelphi Theatre, Baltimore, as Hamlet, Junius Brutus Booth, then lessee of the house, played the part of second actor, and on the delivery of his speech before the prince, the audience rose and cheered him, not only for the beauty of his elocution, but likewise for the modesty which prompted him to represent this subordinate character.

Soon after his return to America in 1827 Booth had undertaken the stage management of the Camp Street Theatre, New Orleans; and here he played Richard III. for sixteen consecutive nights to large audiences. Moreover, having studied the parts of some French dramas, and being sufficiently versed in their language, he played the heroes in the original, giving great delight to a large section of the inhabitants of this city. At the close of his engagement he visited Cincinnati and various other towns, and in 1831 became lessee of the Baltimore Theatre. A short time afterwards, whilst playing at Richmond, news reached him that one of his children was seriously ill, on which, without informing the manager of his intention, he quitted the city and hastened home, where he found the little one dying. A few days more, and the child was interred in the graveyard of the farm. He then resolved to return and end his engagement, but on reaching Baltimore, was informed the Richmond Theatre had closed, and the manager had left for New York. Whilst detained by a heavy fall of snow, he received a letter from the farm asking him to return immediately, as another of his daughters was sick unto death, on which he speedily set out for his home, which he reached just in time to see her expire. Passionately devoted as he was to his children, this double grief unsettled his mind, and for a time darkness fell upon his life.

After an interval he recovered, but the madness which had all along been closely allied to his genius became henceforth more perceptible. Occasionally he quietly and suddenly disappeared from his home, to return after many days, without giving any reason for his absence. He still continued to fulfil engagements all over America, sometimes betraying no eccentricity, and again manifesting strong evidence of his mind's disease.

Once when playing a round of characters at the Boston Theatre, he was announced to act Ludovico in *Evalene*, and a crowded house gathered to see his performance. On his first entrance something unusual was noticed in his voice, manner, and expression. As he proceeded with his part, the audience became aware he was mixing up lines from various plays in a strange and bewildering way. Occasionally he hesitated, ran to the prompter's side of the stage, and lent against the scene whilst his speeches were being audibly spoken. In this manner the two first acts of the tragedy were gone through, the house wondering and fearing greatly; but early in the third act, whilst engaged in conversing with the King of Naples, he broke into a laugh, and departing from the blank verse of his part, and the dignity of his stage tone, said in a colloquial, gossiping manner, "Upon my word, sir; I don't know, sir."

The audience was not less surprised than His Majesty, and a dead silence followed broken by Booth, who, turning to the spectators, continued, "Ladies and gentlemen, I really don't know this part. I studied it only once before, much against my inclination. I will read it, and the play shall go on. By your leave the play shall go on, and Mr. Wilson shall read the part for me." At this point hisses and murmurs rose from the house, at which Booth burst into a ringing laugh. The manager then rushed from behind the scenes and led him off, whilst he shouted out, "I can't read—I am a charity boy; I can't read. Take me to the lunatic asylum." The curtain then fell, and the manager came forward to offer some explanation. It was obvious, he said, that Mr. Booth could not again appear that evening, nor the play proceed. He had been ill on Saturday, but on this day, Monday, was to all appearances quite recovered; indeed he would not have been announced to act that evening had not his physicians stated that he had recovered his powers, and was fully competent to perform. A comedy was then substituted, to the satisfaction of the house.

Poor Booth was taken to his lodgings and carefully attended; but his disorder increasing, it was thought advisable to have a consultation of medical men as to whether he had better be removed to a lunatic asylum. But when the doctors were summoned, it was found the patient had escaped; and on search and inquiry being made, the only tidings which could be obtained of him was, that he had gone to the Marlborough Hotel to engage a place in the Providence stage-coach; but that conveyance having already departed, he disappeared, where none could say. However, on the arrival of a coach from Providence, the driver said he had met Mr. Booth on the road without coat or waistcoat. The following day he arrived at Providence, having neither shoes nor stockings, and at once went to a sailors' boarding-house. Rumour of the popular actor's condition being noised all over the town, his friend Colonel Josiah Jones at once sought him. Booth greeted him kindly, and asked him to take off his boots that he might try them on; and the Colonel, in order to humour him, complying with this request, Booth immediately left the house. Colonel Jones quickly borrowed a pair of shoes, rushed after and overtook him as he hurried along the street in an excited state, and succeeded in persuading him to accompany him home.

Under his watchful care the tragedian in a few days recovered the proper balance of his mind, and was allowed to journey to the farm. But lucid intervals were now succeeded by fits of mental aberration. Soon after he arrived at his home he summoned all his neighbours near and far to attend a funeral, and they, assembling with decent gravity at the appointed day and hour, found it was the carcase of a favourite horse he wished to have buried with solemnity; on which they departed, some in anger, some in sorrow, to their homes.

He was soon before the public again; and in 1838, accompanied by Tom Flynn, manager of the National Theatre, left New York on board the steamer *Neptune* for Charleston. Ten years before, William Conway, who had played Romeo to the Juliet of Miss O'Neill at Covent Garden Theatre, and who subsequently, whilst acting at Bath, became the object of Mrs. Piozzi's affections, had, whilst on his way to Charleston, flung himself into the sea and been drowned. As the ship *Neptune* came towards the spot where 'the unhappy actor was last seen, Booth became exceedingly melancholy, spoke much of Conway, and at last, rushing up on deck, saying that he had a message for him, jumped overboard before it was possible to prevent him. A boat was immediately lowered, and with some danger and difficulty he was rescued. When safe, his first words to Flynn were, "I say, Tom, look out; you're a heavy man, be steady, for if the boat upsets we'll all be drowned."

It was while at Charleston that, in a quarrel with a fellow player, he received a blow from a heavy weapon that broke the bridge of his nose—an incident scarce worth recording, save to note the coincidence that Kean, whom he so strangely and so strongly resembled, mentally and physically, likewise in a squabble was dealt a blow with a pewter pot which disfigured his nose. This accident to Booth threatened permanently to injure his voice as well as his personal appearance;

but instead of giving way to the infirmity he battled strongly against it, continually speaking with all his strength, until, after a lapse of two years, he fully recovered his resonant tones.

And so he continued his life, playing year after year in the principal cities of the States, and then seeking retirement with his family, until 1852, when he spoke of leaving the stage, and gave the jewelled crown he had always worn as Richard III. to his son Edwin whilst they were playing at San Francisco. The time was close at hand when he was to make his exit from life's stage; for a couple of weeks later, whilst on his homeward way, he fell ill of a cold, and died on the 30th of November.

After spending two years and a half in America, Charles Kean returned to England in February, 1833. His father had meanwhile been obliged by illness to abandon all idea of again visiting the States. He therefore rested for some time in his cottage at Bute, but was necessitated in January, 1831, to leave this retreat and again seek engagements; he therefore appeared at Drury Lane, and was warmly welcomed by the public. Seemingly he had benefited by his few months of retirement, but his health was far from being restored. That he was mentally active is proved by his desire to become lessee of the Richmond Theatre, then to be let. He therefore addressed the following letter to the owner—

"*To* Mr. Budd, *Theatre Royal, Richmond, Surrey.*

"*Feb.* 10, 1831.

"Dear Sir,

"Having heard that the Theatre Royal, Richmond, is in the market, I should gladly offer myself as a candidate if I could ascertain to whom I should apply. Its proximity to London would answer my interests in every way, and the fact is, I am weary of scampering about His Majesty's domains, and till I make my final bow to the British Public, I think a good company, well appointed and governed by a man of forty years' theatrical experience, would fix upon my retreat both pleasure and profit. If you would do me the favour to let me know if my name would not be objectionable to the proprietors, or my industry to the public, the rent, taxes, &c., &c., you will confer an obligation on

"Yours truly,

"Edmund Kean.

"P.S.—You will be kind enough to remember that

despatch is the soul of business, and many provincial managers are awaiting my decisions.

"*Kennington Lane, opposite the
Chinese entrance to Vauxhall.*"

Eventually he became lessee of the Richmond Theatre, and took up his residence in the small house attached to the building. The announcement of the fact caused a pleasant sensation amongst playgoers at Richmond and the surrounding neighbourhood, and on nights when he was announced to perform he was at first greeted by crowded audiences. He therefore braced himself to play three times a week, but the novelty of his appearance here wearing gradually away, he acted to poor houses, so that on one occasion the treasury received but three pounds sixteen shillings. Few things gave him more pleasure than to receive his old friends and associates. Here in the cottage sitting-room, with its deep embrasured windows shaded with branches of trailing vines, he talked with them of the past—of those whom they had known, pitied, admired, or loved; the living still amongst them, the departed who were in their midst no more; recalling his victories, forgetting his griefs in the past, welcoming hopes of the future. At times he played to them, or sang Moore's melodies with much of his old expression, and would at their request repeat the Lord's Prayer in a manner which drew tears to their eyes.

Here it was that the veteran actor Henry Howe when a mere lad called to ask advice concerning his becoming a player, of the great man whose performance of Richard III. had a little before fascinated him. At the moment of his visit Kean with his five dogs was about to have himself rowed upon the pleasant Thames, and invited the aspirant for dramatic honours to accompany him, and he complying, Kean entered into conversation with the youth by asking him if he were prepared to starve; and then assured him he himself had sometimes in the course of his life been eighteen or twenty hours without food. Finally, he strove to dissuade the lad from becoming an actor, but, fortunately for a later generation, his advice was not followed.

Occasionally he played at Drury Lane or the Haymarket, receiving fifty pounds a night for each performance. And as his strength decayed, one who knew him relates, "he found it necessary upon nearly every occasion to be supported to the side or wings of the stage, but immediately he was before the public his energy seemed entirely to master all physical weakness, and he would tread the stage with a firmness which would a few minutes previously have seemed impossible." These exertions were followed by prostration.

The genius within him occasionally flamed, and reminded many of his former strength, but more often his acting was dull and mechanical. In this year Fanny Kemble, her father, and her cousin fell to talking one night at supper of Kean. Charles Kemble held no love for the tragedian, and his daughter admits he was "hard upon poor Kean's defects, because they were especially antagonistic to his artistic taste and tendency; but I think too," she adds, "there is a slight infusion of the vexation of unappreciated labour in my father's criticism of Kean." Hers was far more gentle and just; and, coming from one who understood the difficulties besetting an actor's interpretation of his feelings and imagination, are valuable. That he was a man of genius, no matter how he abused his gifts, she was sure; that he possessed the first element of all greatness—power—she was likewise certain, for instinctively, with a word, a look, a gesture, he "tore away the veil from the heart of common humanity, and laid it bare as it beat in every human heart, as it throbbed in his own. Let his deficiencies be what they may, his faults however obvious, his conceptions however erroneous, and his characters, each considered as a whole, however imperfect, he has one atoning faculty that compensates for everything else, that seizes, rivets, electrifies all who see and hear him, and stirs down to their very springs the passionate elements of nature. Genius alone can do this."

His failing health rendered his appearance in public doubtful, even when announced to perform, and he frequently disappointed his audiences; still they crowded the house when he played, knowing their opportunities of seeing him must now be few, and believing they would never look upon his like again. Dr. Doran, who remembered seeing him play Richard III. at the Haymarket in 1832, says the sight was pitiable. " Genius was not traceable in that bloated face ; intellect was all but quenched in those once matchless eyes; and the power seemed gone, despite the will that would recall it. I noted in a diary that night the above facts, and in addition, that by bursts he was as grand as he had ever been, that though he looked well as long as he was still, he moved only with difficulty, using his sword as a stick." Once whilst playing Sir Giles Overreach about this time at Brighton, he fainted in the last act, and was carried off the stage in an insensible condition, moaning the while as if in great pain. On recovering he asked in what part of the performance he had fallen, and being told it was after making a long speech, he whispered, "Ah, I fear it will be my last dying speech."

In the month of November in this year Edmund Kean for the first time acted with Macready. The latter had returned in 1827 from America, where he had been highly successful, and was engaged to play at Drury Lane. In the spring of the following year he had given a series of performances at the Salle Favre, Paris, receiving one hundred pounds a week for three weeks, after which he returned to London. He then made a prolonged tour in the provinces, at the conclusion of which, in 1830, he accepted a fresh engagement at Drury Lane for three years, at a salary of thirty pounds a week and a clear benefit for the first year, and fifty pounds a week for the succeeding years. During this time it was proposed to Kean that Macready should act with him, and the tragedian now consenting to what he had formerly refused, played Othello to Macready's Iago. The latter records in his diary that he acted Iago well, "when Kean did not interfere with me;" but Alfred Bunn, who was now stage-manager at this theatre, has more to say concerning the event. "I was extremely amused," he writes, "with a brief specimen of Shakespearean language addressed to me by both these gentlemen after the curtain fell on their first appearance together in the tragedy of Othello. Kean had a thorough contempt for Macready's acting; and the latter, affecting to be indignant at the mode in which Kean had conducted himself (in always keeping a step or two behind him, whereby the spectators had a full view of the one performer's countenance and only a side view of the other), bounced into my room, and at first vowed he would play with him no more. He finally wound up by saying, 'And pray what is the next p—lay you ex—pect me to appear in—with that low—man.' I replied that I would send him word. I went up into Kean's dressing-room, where I found him scraping the colour off his face, and sustaining the operation by copious draughts of cold brandy-and-water. On my asking him what play he would next appear in with Macready, he ejaculated, 'How the—should I know what the—plays in.'"

Kean's condition was such at this time as to excite the compassion of all who beheld him. Regarding his weakness J. B. Johnston narrates that on one occasion, whilst he was playing the part of Tubal to Kean's Shylock, the latter was so infirm that grave apprehensions were entertained lest he should be unable to finish his representation. However, he struggled hard with his weakness until arriving at the close of the first scene of the third act, where Shylock is wrought to violent rage by the news received of his daughter from Tubal. And here Kean was so overcome by his simulated passion that he greatly feared he would be unable to leave the stage; therefore, instead of ending the scene with the words, "Go, Tubal, and meet me at our synagogue," he tottered forward, and leaning heavily on Johnston said, "Lead me to our synagogue," when the pitying player bore him from the stage. Stooping, dragging his feet after him, gasping for breath, wiping his tears away with a trembling hand, and in his agitation unconsciously twisting his pocket-handkerchief round his fingers, he waited to make his entrances, but once on the boards, his form became erect, and the words he uttered seemed to bear him mechanically through his part. His appearance at the theatre became less and less frequent, and his time was now chiefly passed at Richmond, where he was carefully tended by his old and faithful friend Miss Tidswell, who, after forty years' service at Drury Lane, had retired from the theatre.

Daily he might be seen, wrapped in furs, driving slowly through the peaceful glades of Richmond Park, a pale-faced, worn man, with bright anxious eyes; Miss Tidswell, a grave, gray-haired woman, seated beside him. To her, as to all who knew him, it was clear that, though only in his forty-sixth year, his days were numbered. Intoxicated by the victory which had succeeded struggle, proud of the royal gifts which were his, he had wasted his health and enfeebled his mind, and now drew daily nigh unto death at an age when other men rejoice in the fullness of their strength. 'Twas but as yesterday he had for the first time played Shylock, Richard, and Othello on the Drury Lane stage, whilst all men sounded his praise. Life had then been full of boundless promise; the horizon limiting his hopes had stretched into infinite space, but he had voluntarily squandered his genius and reduced his existence to a span. How foolish now looked his folly; how paltry the treasures for which he had sacrificed so much; how false the friendships in which he had placed strong faith.

Such thoughts must have visited him again and again during his quiet drives through Richmond Park, or during these peaceful evenings, when, after an early dinner, he sat at the piano, singing in a broken voice the songs he had sung of old, whilst tears welled into his eyes and streamed down his cheeks. The feverish excitement of life had subsided for ever, and the end brought peace and regret.

On warm days he would, with slow and languid step, supported by a stick, and accompanied by Miss Tidswell, walk about the green, and here he was met by Helen Faucit, then a little child. The record of her impression presents a picture in itself, and were better read as related in her own choice words. "One of my earliest and vivid recollections—I was then quite a child—was a meeting with 'the great Edmund Kean' as my sister called him. He was her pet hero. She had seen him act, and through friends, had a slight acquaintance with him. Wishing her little 'birdie,' as she often called me, to share all her pleasures, she often took me with her to the green for the chance of seeing him as he strolled there with his aunt, old Miss Tidswell. The great man had been very ill, so that all our expectations had been frequently disappointed. At last about noon one very warm sunny day, my sister's eager eye saw the two figures in the far distance. It would have been bad manners to appear to be watching, so in a roundabout way our approach was made. As we drew near I would gladly have run away. I was startled, frightened at what I saw—a small pale man with a fur cap, and wrapped in a fur cloak. He looked to me as if come from the grave. A stray lock of very dark hair crossed his forehead, under which shone eyes which looked dark, and yet bright as lamps. So large were they, so piercing, so absorbing, I could see no other features. I shrank from them behind my sister, but she whispered to me that it would be unkind to show any fear, so we approached, and were kindly greeted by the pair.

"Oh, what a voice was that which spoke! It seemed to come from far away—a long, long way behind him. After the first salutation, it said, 'Who is this little one?' When my sister had explained, the face smiled (I was reassured by the smile, and the face looked less terrible), and he asked me where I went to school, and which of my books I liked best. Alas! I could not then remember that I liked any, but my ever good angel-sister said she knew I was fond of poetry, for I had just won a prize for recitation. Upon this the face looked still more kindly on me, and we all moved together to a seat under the trees. Then the far-away hollow voice—but it was not harsh—spoke again, as he put his hand in mine, and bade me tell him whether I liked my school walks better than the walks at Richmond. This was too much, and it broke the ice of my silence. No indeed, Greenwich Park was very pretty—so was

Blackheath with its donkeys, when we were, on occasions much too rare, allowed to ride them. But Richmond! Nothing could be so beautiful! I was asked to name my favourite sports, and whether I had ever been in a punt—which I had; and caught fish—which I had not. My tongue, once untied, ran on and on, and had after a time to be stopped, for my sister and the old lady thought I should fatigue the invalid. But he would not part just yet. He asked my name, and when it was told, exclaimed, 'Oh, the old ballad—do you know it?—which begins—

> " Oh, my Helen,
> There is no tellin'
> Why love I fell in ;
> The grave, my dwellin',
> Would I were well in ! "

I know now why with my Helen, love I fell in ; it is because she loves poetry, and she loves Richmond. Will my Helen come and repeat her poetry to me some day ? ' This alarming suggestion at once silenced my prattle, and my sister had to express for me the pleasure and honour I was supposed to feel. Here the interview ended; the kind hand was withdrawn which had lain in mine so heavily, and yet looked so thin and small. I did not know then how great is the weight of weakness. It was put upon my head, and I was bid

God speed! I was to be sent for some day soon. But the day never came; the school-days were at hand. Those wondrous eyes I never saw, and that distant voice I never heard again."

To the inhabitants of Richmond he was an object of interest and pride, whilst the poor regarded him with respect and affection; for no case of distress or poverty was made known to him that he did not strive to relieve. And amongst those to whom his benevolence was extended was his mother's son, Henry Darnley and his family, as may be gathered from a letter written to him by Nance Carey on the 7th of September, 1832.

"DEAR EDMUND,

"I wrote to you the first of this month, my quarter's money being due the 1st of September. As I have had no answer, I fear you did not get my letter. I am in great anxiety till it comes, and being in ill-health makes me feel more. If you can oblige me with two quarters—one due and one in advance—you will render me a very great service. As I may be compelled to remove hastily from the lodging I am now in, I beg you will have the kindness to direct to Mr. Cooper, Surgeon, Great Peter Street, for me, to the care of Mr. Cooper.

"I saw Harry yesterday. His looks are mended since last I saw him. I thank God that you have taken him and his poor chickens under your wing, and I hope you will hold it over them during the winter. I think they have merit, which, cheered by your kindness, will show itself. Mrs. Darnley is clever in Scotch and Irish characters.

"Your affectionate mother,
"M. A. CAREY.

"P.S.—I am in a strange state of health. Two days before I saw Harry every one thought I could not live the night through. I am sorry that I live to trouble my dear child, and yet I cannot wish to die. *Let me see you.*"

With this desire he readily complied, and she not only visited him, but took up her abode under his roof, and remained there till he was laid in his grave.

At the beginning of the year 1833 Edmund Kean, still feeling the necessity of money, had, though struggling with death, entered into an agreement to act a certain number of nights at Drury Lane Theatre, of which Captain Polhill was now lessee. Needing funds immediately, Kean asked Bunn to request

Captain Polhill to lend him five hundred pounds; but the lessee, knowing Kean's circumstances, refused to advance the sum unless security was given for its repayment. Kean promised the money would be paid by his subsequent performances; but the condition of his health being most uncertain, Captain Polhill declined lending him the money. On the 12th of March the tragedian's medical adviser, Mr. James Smith, presented his compliments to Mr. Bunn, and was sorry to inform him "that Mr. Kean is confined by so very severe an attack of gout in his right hand and arm, and some threatening also of the same sort in his legs, as to render it quite impossible for him to perform at present." Mr. Smith added, he would state from day to day how the tragedian progressed; but at present it would be quite impossible to fix any night for his reappearance.

A week later than the date of this note Edmund Kean was advertised to play at Covent Garden Theatre, where Charles Kean was then fulfilling an engagement. It was decided by the management that father and son should play Othello and Iago, and an announcement of this intention caused wide and general interest. Therefore on Monday evening, March 25th, 1833, a great audience assembled to witness Edmund Kean's performance, as it proved, for the last time. Late on that afternoon he had driven to the theatre, and being assisted from his carriage, went at once to his dressing-room, leaving word that he desired to see his son immediately he arrived. Here Charles found him presently, a poor, shrunken figure, with a haggard face and wild eyes, crouching over a fire. He greeted his son affectionately, but said he was very ill, and afraid he should not be able to act. The manager, who was likewise present, cheered him; and having drank some hot brandy and water, he declared he was much better, and allowed himself to be dressed for the part. From time to time he shivered, complained of cold, and to all observers it was evident his vitality was at a low ebb. The sight was pitiful.

Presently, the overture being over, the curtain rose, and Charles Kean, entering as Iago, was warmly greeted. But the audience were evidently impatient for a sight of their old favourite; and when in the second scene he and his son came upon the stage, the whole house received them with the warmest acclamations. Edmund Kean, the tears welling to his eyes, bowed again and again; then suddenly, as if remembering himself, he turned towards Charles, and, taking him by the hand, led him a few steps forward, and, as it were, presented him to the public. At this action the enthusiasm of the house redoubled, hats and handkerchiefs were waved, cheers rent the air, the while father and son stood hand in hand bowing repeatedly. It was a considerable time before they were allowed to proceed with their parts, and then by degrees the feebleness of the great actor's gait and weakness of his voice were noticeable to all; but as it was believed, and hoped, he was reserving his strength for the later acts, no failure was anticipated.

As he came off the stage he remarked, "Charles is getting on well to-night—he's playing very well; I suppose it's because he's acting with me." Again he drank some hot brandy-and-water by way of sustaining his strength, and continued his part in the second act, though his voice was so weak at times that it sank almost to a whisper, and his pauses were longer than usual. It was with a mixture of pain and pleasure the audience followed his acting. Just before the third act began, being fearful his strength would wholly give way, he said to his son, "Mind, Charles, that you keep before me. Don't get behind me in this act; I don't know if I shall be able to kneel, but if I do, be sure that you lift me up." A foreboding of disaster dwelt with him.

HIS LAST PERFORMANCE. 279

With such resolution as he possessed he struggled through the earlier part of the act; but his weakness was greater than his will, and at times he gasped for breath and moved with difficulty, an object of commiseration to all. He continued, however, spoke the lines beginning—

"O now for ever
Farewell the tranquil mind: farewell content;"

and ending with "Farewell: Othello's occupation gone," with all his usual melancholy sweetness, and more than his customary feeling, and so touched and impressed the audience by the sobbing tones of the last line, that they burst into stormy applause that lasted some minutes. Kean stood motionless and fixed, his chin resting on his breast, his eyes riveted upon the ground. A death-like silence, begotten of fear, fell upon the house, feeling which he seemed partially roused to consciousness of the scene, raised his head, and looked round with dimmed sight, advanced a few steps to Iago, and would fain have continued his part, saying, "Villain, be sure—you—prove——" Then, tottering to his son, he flung himself on his neck, and with a faint and faltering voice cried out, "Oh, God, I am dying. Speak to them, Charles." Then one of the other players advanced, and with Charles Kean's assistance carried him off the stage. The public saw him no more.

For hours he lay insensible on a sofa in his dressing-room, his eyes closed as if in death, his limbs motionless and cold, his pulse languid, an anxious crowd of friends and doctors watching him. But by degrees he rallied, and towards midnight he was sufficiently recovered to permit of his being taken to the Wrekin tavern close by, where he lay for upwards of a week 'twixt life and death. At the end of that time he was removed to his house at Richmond, where his secretary, John Lee, and his friend Miss Tidswell, nursed him with untiring devotion. His son, who was obliged to continue his engagement at Covent Garden, was with him daily; and knowing that his father's end was nigh, became anxious a reconciliation should take place between his parents. He therefore suggested to the dying man that he should make his peace with his wife. Accordingly Kean wrote her this last letter—

"MY DEAR MARY,

"Let us be no longer fools. Come home; forget and forgive. If I have erred, it was my head, not my heart, and most severely have I suffered for it. My future life shall be employed in contributing to your happiness; and you, I trust, will return that feeling by a total obliteration of the past.

"Your wild but really affectionate husband,

"EDMUND KEAN.

"*Theatre Royal, Richmond.*"

She to whom it was addressed did not hesitate to obey the request, but immediately drove to Richmond with her son. Leaving her at the Greyhound Hotel, Charles hastened to prepare his father for her visit. Then they who had been parted for eight years met, and words of penitence and forgiveness were spoken; but the shock which his appearance, telling too plainly the certain approach of death, gave Mrs. Kean was great, and after an effort to muster her feelings, she completely broke down, and sobbed piteously. He who heard her knew the cause of her tears, and learned too late the depth of the affection he had discarded. Taking her hand, with a pathetic effort at cheerfulness, he said, "Come, bear up, bear up; happiness shall yet be ours." But though he spoke as if with hope, he knew the sands of his life had almost run. Mrs. Kean, who was now an invalid, returned to town in the evening, but visited him continually.

At times, when he felt better, he still hoped his existence might be prolonged, but more frequently, when overcome by pain and weakness, he feared his end had come. One day early in May, when Douchez, the famous surgeon, drove from town to visit him, he said, "Now, this is very kind of you, but I feel that the hand of death is upon me," and he burst into tears. For some time past he had experienced a disinclination to eat solid food, and he now mainly subsisted on arrowroot and jelly, mixed with brandy-and-water. His son was constantly in attendance on him, and he welcomed the visits of his theatrical friends. The talk of the town, which they narrated to him, and the reminiscences they recalled, excited him, and he seemed to regain much of his former buoyancy in their presence; but they being gone, he frequently fell into a lethargy from which it was difficult to rouse him.

When his old friend Jack Hughes said to him that brighter days were in store for him, he made answer they had passed for ever; and then, his mind wandering, he quoted some lines from a play, and mentioned the names of several singers who had, he stated, promised to come and sing him to sleep, for he was tired. From that day he suffered at intervals from aberration of the mind; at such moments he lived his old life once more—now was he a strolling player struggling for bread, acting in barns, painfully toiling along dreary, interminable roads; and again he was on the stage of Drury Lane, before an audience that greeted him with laudations, or howled at him in fury. And the names of Lord Byron, Whitbread, Rae, and others gone before came familiarly to his lips. That dark passage in his life relating to a woman's infidelity, from which all other evils seemed to follow, were forgotten at such times, and he was back in the morning of his years, when life held fair promises before him.

The early days of May waned, and looking through his bed-room windows, he rejoiced in the new-born spring, which he was not destined to see deepen to the fullness of summer. Pale-faced and attenuated, the ghost of his former self, he sat in bed propped up by pillows, surrounded by books and papers, which he opened one by one, and then wearily laid aside. Occasionally he was strong enough to rise, and was supported into his sitting-room, where he lay on a sofa, or seated at the piano, struck a few chords, to which he listened dreamily, as if they recalled dead memories, and then with trembling limbs and tearful eyes turned away.

But his last days were not allowed to pass in

uninterrupted peace, being intruded on by his creditors. His books showed him to have earned at an average almost ten thousand a year since his first appearance at Drury Lane—a sum three times greater than that gained by any of his contemporary actors. But of this nothing was left; his reckless extravagance had wasted his wealth, and only a few days before his death he was in danger of being arrested for a sum not exceeding one hundred pounds; and after his demise, his theatrical wardrobe and properties, the valuable presents given him, together with the plate and furniture at his cottages in Bute and Richmond, were seized by his creditors and sold, the whole realizing but six hundred pounds.

As May wore on, his weakness increased, and his periods of delirium became longer. Through long silent nights he moaned in pain; he slept through days when sunshine steeped the land. On the evening of Tuesday the 14th he was quite unconscious of those around him. His mind wandering, he held conversation with persons he believed standing by him, the living and the dead; spoke some lines from the plays in which he had won repute, and towards midnight, before those who watched could hinder him, he suddenly jumped from his bed, and crying out in the words of Richard III.—" A horse, a horse, my kingdom for a horse!" fell on his knees. Being put to bed, he passed into a lethargic state. It was nine o'clock in the morning when he woke, and turned his eyes wistfully towards the light, then rested them on the faces of his secretary and the surgeon. Recognizing them, he strove to speak, but though they bent over him, no words fell upon their ears; then quickly and fearfully he flung out his arms, caught their hands, sighed, and was dead.

Ten days later his remains were borne to old Richmond church. His friends had applied to the Dean and Chapter of Westminster Abbey to forego the customary fees, and allow his ashes to rest beside those of Garrick; but this being refused by these reverend gentlemen, his body was placed near the western portal of old Richmond church, close by the bones of Thompson the poet, and not far removed from those of Shakespeare's friend, Burbage, the original representative of Richard III. Every possible mark of respect was shown him. Members of the theatrical profession, not only from London, but from the provinces, alike famous and obscure, accompanied him on his last brief journey. Crowds of mourners filled the village, shops were shut, the funeral service was impressively read, and with the words, "His body is buried in peace, but his name shall live for ever," ringing in their ears, the living parted from the dead. His son erected to his memory a tablet, having a medallion portrait, and bearing these words—

Edmund Kean,

DIED MAY 15, 1833,

AGED 46.

—✠—

A Memorial erected by his Son,

CHARLES JOHN KEAN,

1839.

Richard Clay and Sons, Limited, London and Bungay.

CHEAP EDITIONS OF
POPULAR WORKS
By J. FITZGERALD MOLLOY.

Court Life Below Stairs; or, London under the First Georges.
    Fifth Edition, Crown 8vo., 6s.

Court Life Below Stairs; or, London under the Last Georges.
    Fifth Edition, Crown 8vo., 6s.

The Life and Adventures of Peg Woffington.
    Third Edition, Crown 8vo., 6s.

Royalty Restored; or, London under Charles II.
    Third Edition, Crown 8vo., 6s.

Famous Plays; with a Discourse on the Playhouses of the Restoration.
    Third Edition, Crown 8vo., 6s.

That Villain Romeo; a Novel of Bohemian Life.
    In Picture Boards, 2s.

What Hast Thou Done? a Novel.
    In Picture Boards, 2s.

A Modern Magician; a Novel.
    In Picture Boards, 2s. (In October.)

WARD & DOWNEY, Publishers,
12, YORK STREET, COVENT GARDEN, LONDON.

NOW READY, IN PICTURE BOARDS, PRICE 2s.

WHAT HAST THOU DONE?

"Fitzmaurice the adventurer is finely drawn. We always read the descriptions and the dialogue with pleasure. The humour is better than the sentiment; but we always recognize the work of a practised and facile pen."—*Spectator.*

"This very clever story is far above the average of such productions. The descriptions of Irish life are especially good."—*St. James's Gazette.*

"Mr. Fitzgerald Molloy has written one of the pleasantest and most readable of Irish novels we have lately seen. As a whole it is quite the best we have seen by the author."—*Daily News.*

"The book contains scenes in Bohemian life, scenes in high life in London, and scenes in Ireland. It is bright, picturesque, and entertaining."—*County Gentleman.*

"This novel displays considerable ability. The scenes in which we are introduced to the vanities and follies of society are admirably contrived, and sketched with a firm and true hand."—*Morning Post.*

NOW READY, IN PICTURE BOARDS, PRICE 2s.

THAT VILLAIN ROMEO.

"Few society stories possess the merit of 'That Villain Romeo.' The principal charm in Mr. Molloy's novel is the complex and picturesque study of his heroine. Nothing more piquant and fascinating was ever painted than Marcus Phillip's model. His weird sketches of Bohemia, and his bright, incisive style will suffice to ensure the success to this novel."—*Morning Post.*

"A bright and unquestionably interesting story; not without passages of pungent sarcasm, sometimes tinged with cynicism."—*Academy.*

"An exceedingly powerful and fascinating story. There is much power in the scenes where Capri's own peculiar character, half-poetic, half-worldly is brought out; and the contest between her and her father is well managed. . . . As a drama of inexorable fate the work must rank high."—*Daily Telegraph.*

"The driest and boniest of reviewers will scarcely be able to deny that Mr. Molloy can write in a pleasant style, and describe contemporary society in a manner which, if a little free, is undoubtedly easy. He displays a considerable power of distinct character drawing."—*Daily News.*

WARD & DOWNEY, PUBLISHERS,
12, YORK STREET, COVENT GARDEN, LONDON.

POPULAR WORKS BY THE SAME AUTHOR.

COURT LIFE BELOW STAIRS;

OR,

LONDON UNDER THE FIRST GEORGES.

By J. FITZGERALD MOLLOY.

Crown 8vo., 6s.

FIFTH EDITION.

"No truer or more vivid picture of the last century has been written. The value of the present work as a picture of Court manners under the first Georges is greatly enhanced by the fact that, as far as possible, it is historically correct."—*Morning Post.*

"Mr. Molloy's pages contain abundance of amusing anecdote. He writes in a brisk and fluent style."—*Athenæum.*

"Mr. Molloy produces some curious anecdotes which have not before appeared in print, and he is always lively."—*Pall Mall Gazette.*

"Concerning the amusing incidents and royal quarrels, the domestic scenes, the brilliant and immoral courtiers he has much to say, and, moreover, says it in a witty and pleasant manner. The anecdotes of Pope and Addison, Swift and Steele, Colley Cibber, Gay, Congreve, Susanna Centlivre, Lady Mary Wortley Montagu, and others are all interesting."—*Sunday Times.*

"Though Mr. Molloy has not been alone in recognizing the value of the Wentworth correspondence, it has been for the first time brought by him before the notice of the general public, and his quotations cannot fail to awaken genuine interest. .... In these sketches of Court Life there is no lack of rollicking vivacity to carry the reader along interested in the narrative."—*Academy.*

"Mr. Molloy has evidently found a subject congenial to his taste and fitting to his lively and facile pen."—*Daily News.*

"Well written, full of anecdote, and with its facts admirably grouped, this excellent work will prove of the greatest value to all who desire to know what manner of men the first Electors of Hanover who came here really were. .... Contemporary history of the time treated of is so interwoven that the record is one complete and happily-framed narrative. .... In fine, Mr. Molloy's work as a history seems all that it should be."—*Daily Telegraph.*

WARD & DOWNEY, PUBLISHERS,
12, YORK STREET, COVENT GARDEN, LONDON.

COURT LIFE BELOW STAIRS;
OR,
LONDON UNDER THE LAST GEORGES.
By J. FITZGERALD MOLLOY,
AUTHOR OF "ROYALTY RESTORED."
Crown 8vo., 6s.

"These volumes must be regarded as a valuable contribution to literature; presenting as they do a series of clever, graphic and reliable pictures of the court and social life under the last Georges."—*Sunday Times.*

"Mr. Molloy's style is crisp, and carries the reader along; his portraits of the famous men and women of the time are etched with care, and his narrative rises to intensity and dramatic impressiveness as he follows the latter days of Queen Caroline."—*British Quarterly Review.*

"Mr. Molloy's style is bright and fluent, picturesque and animated, and he tells his story with unquestionable skill and vivacity."—*Athenæum.*

"The narrative is fluent and amusing, and is far more instructive than nine-tenths of the novels published nowadays."—*St. James's Gazette.*

"Mr. Molloy's narrative is concise, and exhibits a wide acquaintance with the men and manners of the age. The anecdotes of the famous men of fashion, wits, fools, or knaves introduced are amusing, and several not generally known enliven the pages."—*Morning Post.*

"Well written, full of facts bearing on every subject under consideration, and abounding with anecdotes of gay and witty debauchees."—*Daily Telegraph.*

"What Pepys has done for the Stuarts, Mr. Molloy has done for their Hanoverian successors. This result of his arduous investigations is one of the most interesting works which has ever come under our notice. It is impossible to open the books at any part without feeling an overpowering desire to continue the perusal."—*Newcastle Chronicle.*

FAMOUS PLAYS.
Crown 8vo., 6s.

"Mr. Fitzgerald Molloy is an earnest and indefatigable author of books, particularly interesting to students of the History of the Drama."—*Punch.*

"Apart from the value of a record so full and exhaustive, it is an interesting study to watch the play of individuality in each of the different authors during the several stages of his pieces, and not less entertaining to follow the train of events leading up to the actual production in each case. Here of course scope exists for Mr. Molloy to make a very palatable dish of small circumstances, reminiscent of wits and men of parts other than those immediately concerned. In a word, 'Famous Plays' is a well written, lively, and thoroughly satisfactory piece of work, which is most worthy of Mr. Molloy's reputation as a stage historian of research and erudition, and an elegant and scholarly writer."—*Stage.*

"By such as prefer the records of an honourable and artistic past to the reports of a garish and blatant present, this odd rehabilitation of unremembered things will be greatly and carefully treasured."—*Vanity Fair.*

"Gives a good idea of the English drama as it existed at certain well-defined periods of its history. . . . The result is a book of a very interesting character, and one that is likely to be much read."—*St. James's Gazette.*

"The story of each of these pieces is not merely an account of its literary genesis, its dramatic production, and its quality and character from the standpoint of the critic or the manager; it is a delightfully gossipy sketch of life and character, manners, fortunes, and adventures. Mr. Molloy has a wonderful gift of revitalizing the past."—*Irish Times.*

WARD & DOWNEY, PUBLISHERS,
12, YORK STREET, COVENT GARDEN, LONDON.

ROYALTY RESTORED;

OR,

LONDON UNDER CHARLES II.

By J. FITZGERALD MOLLOY.

Third Edition, 1 vol., Crown 8vo.

"The most important historical work yet achieved by its author. .... It has remained for a picturesque historian to achieve such a work in its entirety and to tell a tale as it has never before been told."—*Daily Telegraph.*

"A series of pictures carefully drawn, well composed, and correct in all details. Mr. Molloy writes pleasantly, and his book is thoroughly entertaining."—*Graphic.*

"Presents us for the first time with a complete description of the social habits of the period."—*Globe.*

"We are quite prepared to recognize in it the brisk and fluent style, the ease of narration, and other qualities of a like nature, which, as was pointed out in this journal, characterized his former books."—*Athenæum.*

"The story of Charles's marriage, of the prodigious dowry, of the young Queen's innocence of the ways of his world, her wrongs, her sufferings, her brief resistance, her long, lamentable acquiescence, her unfailing love, is well told in this book. Whenever, in its pages, we catch sight of Catherine, it is a relief from the vile company that crowds them, the shameless women and the contemptible men on whom 'the fountain of honour' lavished distinctions, which ought from thenceforth to have lost all meaning and attraction for honest folk. The author has studied his subjects with care and industry; he reproduces them either singly or in groups, with vivid and stirring effect; the comedy and the tragedy of the Court-life move side by side in his chapters. .... A chapter on the Plague is admirable,—impressive without any fine writing: the description of the Fire is better still. To Mr. Molloy's narrative of the Titus Oates episode striking merit must be accorded; also to the closing chapter of the work with its picture of the hard death of King Charles."—*Spectator.*

"In 'Royalty Restored; or, London under Charles II.' Mr. J. Fitzgerald Molloy makes a remarkable advance beyond his preceding works in style and literary method. His book, which is the best, may very well be the last on the subject. ... The shrewdness, the cynicism, and the profound egotism of the Merry Monarch are dexterously conveyed in this picture of him, and the book is variously and vividly interesting."—*World.*

"The author of 'Royalty Restored' has never offered the public so graphic, so fascinating, so charming an example of faded lives revivified, and dim scenes revitalized by the magic of the picturesque historic sense."—*Boston Literary World.*

"Mr. Molloy has not confined himself to an account of the King and his courtiers. He has given us a study of London during his reign, taken, as far as possible, from rare and invariably authentic sources. We can easily see that a work such as this, in order to be successful, must be the result of the most careful study and the most untiring diligence in the consultation of diaries, records, memoirs, letters, pamphlets, tracts, and papers left by contemporaries familiar with the Court and the Capital. There can be no doubt that Mr. Molloy's book bears evidence on every page of such study and diligence."—*Glasgow Evening News.*

"In his delineation of Charles, Mr. Molloy is very successful. ... He avoids vivid colouring; yet rouses our interest and sympathy with a skilful hand."—*St. James's Gazette.*

WARD & DOWNEY, Publishers,
12, YORK STREET, COVENT GARDEN, LONDON.

THE LIFE AND ADVENTURES OF
PEG WOFFINGTON.

Third Edition, Crown 8vo., 6s.

"The work is a theatrical and literary history of the period, with a most attractive central figure, on whom Mr. Molloy is careful to keep as full and steady a light as possible. Round the heroine are set successions of changing groups, skilfully ranged and posed—Dr. Johnson and Goldsmith amongst authors; Barry, Quin, and Macklin amongst actors; Rich and Colley Cibber amongst managers; while the men of the world of that date, dandified and costly and boasting, are well ranged as accessories. The book is like a succession of scenes as were to be witnessed in the olden days, with all the delicacy, brilliancy and dash in the individual figures; and also with all the suggestions of hollowness and superficiality and sentiment and gallantry that marked the era. The pages sparkle with well-chosen anecdotes, and the reader is carried on from page to page, as in the case of a well-constructed fiction."—*British Quarterly.*

"In dealing with the literary and dramatic personages of her time, and with the general society of the period, Mr. Molloy is a faithful chronicler, and faithful not only in spirit, but also as to facts. There is not a prominent personage about whom a number of characteristic anecdotes are not told."—*St. James's Gazette.*

"This book has the merit of being, from the first chapter to the last, without a single dull page."—*Daily News.*

"Mr. Molloy's book presents the best and most readable life of Peg Woffington that has been produced."—*Scotsman.*

"Peg Woffington makes a most interesting central figure, round which Mr. Fitzgerald Molloy has made to revolve a varied and picturesque panorama of London life in the middle of the eighteenth century."—*Illustrated London News.*

A MODERN MAGICIAN.

In picture boards 2s. (*In October.*)

"We find a very good plot and some clever sketches of types and individuals belonging to the most modern phase of society. The hero and heroine are interesting, and the inconsistency of each in his kind and her several ways is true to life: it is, however, a new departure for a novelist to depict this moral defect with such startling frankness and results so terrible."—*Spectator.*

"Sometimes a portrait is painted in a single sentence, and every character is forcibly drawn. . . . Mr. Molloy is a poet, and some of his descriptions linger long in the reader's memory."—*Boston Herald.*

"Mr. Fitzgerald Molloy takes the reader with him without pause, from first page to last, by virtue of the interest felt in his hero and heroine."—*Globe.*

"The entire book shows a series of daring and original scenes which set it quite apart from the ordinary novel. In his quality of a practised novelist, Mr. Molloy has produced a work that will claim the ready adhesion of the believers in mysticism, whilst its forcibly-drawn characters and striking incidents will suit the taste of the admirers of realistic fiction. In fact the two absolutely opposing elements of occultism and realism are in these pages made to mingle in a fashion that has not previously been attempted."—*Morning Post.*

"A striking work of fiction. . . . There is a capital garniture of society life, of good dialogue, of the lives of worthy people. The novel will be found more interesting and far abler than most stories of the day."—*Scotsman.*

WARD & DOWNEY, PUBLISHERS,
12, YORK STREET, COVENT GARDEN, LONDON.

www.ingramcontent.com/pod-product-compliance
Lightning Source LLC
Chambersburg PA
CBHW032047230426
43672CB00009B/1509